Fishes
of the
COLUMBIA BASIN

*A guide to their natural
history and identification*

Dennis D. Dauble

Sandpoint, Idaho

Keokee Books, Sandpoint, Idaho 83864

© 2009 by Dennis D. Dauble. Photos by author unless otherwise noted

All rights reserved. No part of this book may be reproduced in any manner without the express written consent of the publisher, except in the case of brief excerpts in critical reviews and articles.

Printed in the United States of America

Published by Keokee Books, an imprint of Keokee Co. Publishing, Inc.
P.O. Box 722
Sandpoint, ID 83864
208-263-3573

www.KeokeeBooks.com

Publisher's Cataloging-in-Publication Data

Dauble, Dennis D.
    Fishes of the Columbia Basin: a guide to their natural history and identification / Dennis D. Dauble
    Includes bibliographic references.
    Includes index.
    1. Fishes–Columbia River Basin 2. Fishes–Columbia River Basin–Identification 3. Fishes–Columbia River Basin–Environmental Aspects.
    597.0979
ISBN 978-1-879628-34-2

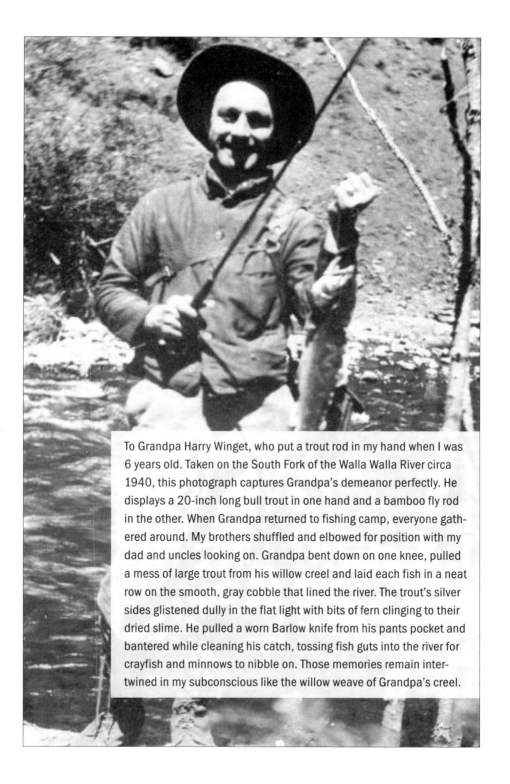

To Grandpa Harry Winget, who put a trout rod in my hand when I was 6 years old. Taken on the South Fork of the Walla Walla River circa 1940, this photograph captures Grandpa's demeanor perfectly. He displays a 20-inch long bull trout in one hand and a bamboo fly rod in the other. When Grandpa returned to fishing camp, everyone gathered around. My brothers shuffled and elbowed for position with my dad and uncles looking on. Grandpa bent down on one knee, pulled a mess of large trout from his willow creel and laid each fish in a neat row on the smooth, gray cobble that lined the river. The trout's silver sides glistened dully in the flat light with bits of fern clinging to their dried slime. He pulled a worn Barlow knife from his pants pocket and bantered while cleaning his catch, tossing fish guts into the river for crayfish and minnows to nibble on. Those memories remain intertwined in my subconscious like the willow weave of Grandpa's creel.

Contents

Introduction vi
Acknowledgments viii

1. The Great Columbia River Plain   1
Regional Landscape 2
Rivers, Streams and other Waterways 3
Human Development Activities 7

2. History of Fish Use in the Columbia River   13
American Indian Lifestyles 13
Commercial and Sport Harvest of Fishes 20
Introduction of Non-Native Fishes 28

3. Studies of Columbia Basin Fishes   31
Early Explorers to the Region (1805-1850) 32
First Scientific Expeditions (1840-1900) 39
Modern Fisheries Science 42

4. Ecology and Behavior of Fishes   45
Aquatic Food Webs 46
Life History Strategies 48
Species Interactions 55

5. Environmental Factors Affecting Fish Distribution and Abundance   59
Water Temperature 59
Dissolved Oxygen 61
Discharge 62
Substrate 65
Salinity 66
Water Quality 67

6. How to Identify Fishes   71
Care and Handling of Fishes 72
Observing Fishes 72
General Features of Fishes 73
External Anatomy 74
Internal Anatomy 78

How to Count and Measure...80

7. Key to Common Fishes of the Region   85
Key to Families 86
Key to Individual Species 94

8. Biology of Columbia Basin Fishes   109
Lampreys 109
Sturgeons...112
Herrings 115
Trout, Salmon, Chars and Whitefishes 116
Smelts 134
Pikes...134
Minnows..136
Suckers...145
Catfishes...149
Killifishes 154
Live-bearers 154
Cods 155
Sticklebacks..156
Trout-perches 157
Bass and Sunfishes 158
Perches...164
Sculpins 167

REFERENCES 171

APPENDIXES
Appendix A. Glossary of Terms 182
Appendix B. List of Fishes by Family 185
Appendix C. Location of Columbia River Tributaries and Dams 188
Appendix D. Regional Web Sites Related to Fish and Fishing....................190

INDEX...192

Introduction

The primary purpose of this book is to describe the natural history of fishes commonly found in the Columbia Basin of Oregon and Washington. In addition to being a guide to the identification of more than 60 species of fish, it provides facts on their distribution, relative abundance and life history. This guide will help answer questions such as "What kind of fish is that?," "How big do they get?" and "What do they eat?" It also provides information on fish behaviors that will help anglers figure out where, when and how to catch them.

•••

I was lucky enough early in my scientific career to have a job that allowed me to collect fishes from the Columbia and Snake rivers. Having the opportunity to study fish in their natural habitat and in the laboratory has given me a greater understanding of their life history and behavior. I have also drawn upon research and teaching experience to provide information on topics of interest to sportsmen, nature lovers, students and fisheries scientists. A broad view was considered because fishes are important for more reasons than fishing. Fishes are part of American Indian culture, they are good to eat and they live in interesting places, to name a few.

The region of interest is the interior Columbia River Basin. The fish I describe reside in the Columbia River between Lake Roosevelt and the mouth of the Willamette River. They frequent the lower Snake River, inland waterways of eastern Washington, and streams that flow from the Blue Mountains and eastern slopes of the Cascades in Washington and Oregon.

Rather than focus solely on individual fishes and their biology, I first provide a context for fishes and their way of life. Thus, the book has two parts, each with different emphases. The first part, chapters 1 to 5, provides the geographical, historical and environmental context for fishes that inhabit the Columbia Basin. Chapter 1 begins with a description of the regional landscape, including the different waterways where fishes reside and the human development activities that have impacted these populations. Chapter 2 describes the history of fishing in the Columbia Basin, from American Indians through current commercial and sport harvest. Chapter 3 includes early accounts of fishes from the journals of explorers in the region and the first scientific studies of fishes in the Columbia and Snake rivers. Chapter 4 is an introduction to aquatic ecology. It describes food webs and the life-history strategies of common fishes. Factors that influence the distribution and abundance of fishes are emphasized in chapter 5.

The second part of the book is intended as a guide to identifying common fishes of the Columbia Basin. Chapter 6 shows what characteristics to look for to distinguish one fish from another. Chapter 7 is a key that allows one to identify the most common species known or expected to occur in this region. Chapter 8 is the longest. It serves as a reference to the basic biology of fishes found in the region. Also included is a comprehensive species list, color plates of the most commonly encountered fishes, and additional references for readers interested in exploring individual species in more detail. Much of the information contained in the book is applicable to fishes found throughout the Inland Northwest.

I hope this book will be stored in your tackle box as a ready guide to fishes that you catch or encounter while wading or snorkeling in inland waterways. It should be taken along during excursions to rivers and lakes, similar to a favorite shirt or hat. Alternatively, it should be placed next to the bedside or on the shelf along with other outdoor reference books. Dog-ear the pages to readily locate a favorite species of fish, let it get water-stained and write notes in it. Memorize fish facts and use the knowledge to impress your friends and relatives. Life is too short for anyone not to have a book on fishes.

Acknowledgments

Many individuals deserve credit for their support in completing this project. I thank my parents for letting me play in "cricks" and raising me to be both curious and critical. I am also indebted to my wife, Nancy, and our two grown children, Diana and Matt, for their tolerance of my passion for fish and fishing. Professors Carl Bond, Charles Warren and Larry Curtis from Oregon State University were each influential in teaching about fishes in ways that were intellectual and practical. For this I am grateful. I thank C. Dale Becker, Don Watson, Robert Gray and Thomas Page from Pacific Northwest National Laboratory who served as mentors throughout much of my professional career.

Supporting illustrations in chapters 6 and 7 are from Carl Bond's *Keys to Oregon Freshwater Fishes* and C.J.D. Brown's *Fishes of Montana*. Permission to use the color photographs from *Inland Fishes of Washington* was generously provided by Richard Whitney. The banded killifish and tadpole madtom pictures were taken by John Sarcola and Bill Pflieger, respectively. I also thank Deward Walker, Eugene Hunn, James Keyser, American Fisheries Society, the Stark Museum of Art, Oregon State University Press, University of Washington, Washington State Historical Society, University of Oregon Libraries and Northwestern University Library for allowing me to use artwork and images from their works. All figures are from sources identified in the main body, where appropriate.

For the latter half of the book, I relied heavily on information from *The Freshwater Fishes of British Columbia* by Carl, Clemens and Lindsey (1967); *Freshwater Fishes of Canada* (1973) by Scott and Crossman Wydoski; *Bond's Keys to Oregon Freshwater Fishes* (1973); *Fishes of Idaho* (1982) by Simpson and Wallace; and Wydowski and Whitney's *Inland Fishes of Washington* (2003). This information was supplemented with research reports and scientific literature.

Finding the inspiration and time to write is one thing, finishing the task is another. It is only through the assistance of friends and colleagues that I got to an end point. Georganne O'Connor deserves credit for encouraging me to write outside of the mold of a practicing scientist. Her insight to the importance of story has been invaluable. C. Dale Becker donated many hours to review and edit this book, correcting challenges with grammar. Those that remain are mine. I thank Jack Nisbet for sharing his knowledge of the natural history of the region and providing a whole new context for understanding fishes. I also thank David Geist,

Geoff McMichael, Mark Freshley, Darby Stapp, Janelle Downs and Bruce Bjornstad who reviewed different chapters. They helped set me straight on facts and advised on how to present them. My daughter-in-law, Julianna Dauble, and wife, Nancy, improved presentation of material in chapters 6 and 7. Darlene Mahon assisted with word processing challenges. Finally, I thank Ann Lamott for sharing how to get a grip on writing in the instructional novel *Bird by Bird*. Much of this book was written fish by fish.

•••

"The concavity of surface and girdling highlands have given a special character to the two great rivers, the Columbia and the Snake, which join near the center of the Plain."
—D.W. Meinig, *The Great Columbia Plain*, 1968

The Snake River is a major tributary of the Columbia River in the U.S. states of Wyoming, Idaho, Oregon and Washington.

"In a sense, two Columbia Rivers flow through our lives – the river we see today and the natural river that gave rise to the spectacular sights and thunderings of such places as Celilo and Kettle Falls."
—William D. Layman,
River of Memory: The Everlasting Columbia, 2006

Chapter 1. The Great Columbia River Plain

The general setting for this book includes a region once known as the Great Columbia Plain, a place unlike any other in the United States (Figure 1.1). It has steep river valleys, broad floodplains, rolling grassland, and barren and rocky slopes known as scabland. Within this region are the streams, rivers and lakes that make up most of the interior Columbia Basin. These waterways support diverse fish populations held in high regard by their inhabitants and the thousands of people who visit the region annually.

So, why care about fishes from the Columbia Basin? I know that I am not alone in a quest for fishes and places where they live. But, it's not all about fishing. To many people, it's enough to know there are places where fishes reside, that waterways are not so polluted that future generations will be deprived, or that they too could angle for a dinner of rainbow trout if they wished. Residents of the Inland Northwest are serious about fish and fishing. However, before attempting to convince readers about the importance of fishes, I describe the backdrop of the Columbia Basin, for features of the land and the water cycle dictate where fishes exist.

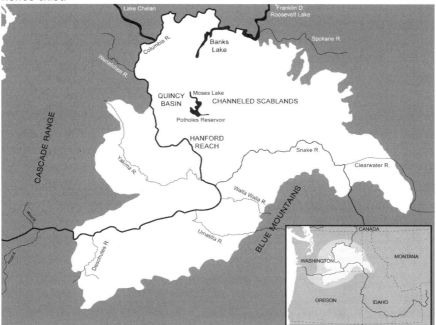

Figure 1.1. Geographic range for fishes of the Columbia Basin (modified from D.W. Meinig, *The Great Columbia River Plain*. Seattle, 1995)

Regional Landscape

The interior Columbia Basin is relatively flat, with elevations ranging from about 200 feet to 2,500 feet above sea level. Volcanic Columbia River basalt is the prominent rock type of the region. Much of the current landscape was formed by ancient lava flows that began around 17 million years to 6 million years ago. Since that time, river and lake deposits of the Ringold Formation partially filled the basin. Catastrophic events such as the Ice Age floods helped shape the drainage as far east as the Palouse Slope by carving down to underlying bedrock. The Bonneville flood also shaped the landscape from the east via the Snake River. These ancient floods created flow paths for rivers and sculpted out low spots to create inland lakes. Over time, fishes colonized different habitats as the lakes and rivers shifted under the influence of ancient cataclysms.

Since the Ice Age, riverbeds of coarse gravel have formed along the Columbia and Snake rivers, creating important production areas for fishes. Buildup of river gravel is especially common at the confluence of the Clearwater and Snake rivers and where large tributaries – including the Wenatchee, Yakima, Snake and Deschutes rivers – enter the Columbia River. Unfortunately, backwaters of hydroelectric dams now inundate many of these entry points.

Figure 1.2. John Day Rapids (Washington State Historical Society, Asahel Curtis, Plate 54970)

It is hard to imagine that several rapids and falls existed in the Columbia and Snake rivers. The Columbia River at Priest Rapids once dropped 73 feet in 11 miles. The Umatilla Rapids, downstream of Wallula Gap, as well as several sets of rapids near the present site of Ice Harbor Dam on the lower Snake River, were also treacherous to early steamboats and other river travelers (Figure 1.2).

These rapids paled in comparison to the thundering waters of Kettle and Celilo falls that framed the upper and lower portions of the interior Columbia Basin. Much of the interior Columbia Basin is dry, receiving only 6 to 10 inches of precipitation per year. Most rainfall occurs in the winter. Predominant upland vegetation is big sagebrush, rabbitbrush and bunchgrass. There is little riparian vegetation along the banks of the Columbia and Snake rivers. Occasional cottonwood and black locust provide roost sites for fish-loving osprey, bald eagle and great blue heron. Juniper and pine trees grace the hillsides at the northern end of the Great Columbia Plain. Only the upper sections of tributary streams provide glimpses of fir and alder.

The Cascade Range bounds the western part of the basin, or the lower Columbia River. Here, where rainfall is higher, scattered stands of conifer mixed with oak may be found. The river gorge widens downstream of Bonneville Dam as basalt cliffs give way to broad lowlands and terraces.

Rivers, Streams and Other Waterways

The Columbia River is one of the largest rivers in North America, ranking fifth in drainage area and third in total discharge. Its source is Columbia Lake, in the Canadian Rockies, nearly 1,240 river miles from the Pacific Ocean. From that point, the Columbia River drops gradually 2,650 feet in elevation and flows through several climatic zones, ranging from alpine to shrub steppe. The Columbia River drains 259,000 square miles, with most of its watershed in the United States. Seasonal runoff patterns for the myriad of tributaries that feed the Columbia River system are largely driven by snowmelt. Fish populations in tributaries are generally less diverse and consist mostly of native species, except in lower reaches inundated by backwater of dams.

The Snake River is the largest tributary in the Columbia River drainage. It flows almost 1,700 miles from its source deep in the Rockies. The final 100 miles of the lower Snake River meander westward from Lewiston, Idaho, before entering the Columbia River at Pasco, Washington, near the center of the Great Columbia Plain. Flows in the Snake River average about 20 percent of the Columbia River. The

Clearwater River joins the Snake River at Lewiston, approximately 140 miles above the confluence. Its watershed extends about 10,000 square miles. Tributaries of the lower Snake River downstream of the Clearwater River include the Tucannon and Palouse rivers. The lower Snake River is a series of reservoirs created by four hydroelectric dams.

Significant tributary streams of the Columbia River, in a downstream direction from Lake Roosevelt, include the Spokane, Okanogan, Methow, Entiat, Wenatchee, Yakima, Walla Walla, Umatilla, John Day, Deschutes, Klickitat, Hood, White Salmon, Wind, Sandy and Willamette rivers (Figure 1.3). The Willamette River is Oregon's largest river with a basin area of 28,800 square kilometers. The lower 20 miles are tidal to Willamette Falls. Much of the river has been modified for navigation, flood control and hydroelectric development.

Figure 1.3. Upper Yakima River (author photo)

The Columbia and Snake rivers can be segregated into mid-Columbia River reservoirs upstream of Priest Rapids Dam, the lower Columbia River downstream of McNary Dam and the lower Snake River. Mid-Columbia River reservoirs are cooler than reservoirs of the lower Snake and lower Columbia rivers. Thus, the number and abundance of warmwater-tolerant fishes is reduced. The lower Columbia River has more discharge and a lower gradient. The abundant backwaters there favor introduced species such as walleye and bass. Bonneville Dam, 146 miles from the Pacific Ocean, serves as a migration barrier for many fishes. The lower Snake River is warmest and has few tributary streams. Channel catfish, bass and sunfishes thrive there, along with abundant minnows and suckers.

Two large reservoirs, Franklin D. Roosevelt Lake and Banks Lake, reside at the upper end of the U.S. portion of the Columbia Basin. Lake Roosevelt extends 150 miles upstream from Grand Coulee Dam nearly to the Canadian border. More than 2.5 million acre-feet of water are pumped from Lake Roosevelt annually into the 30-mile-long Banks Lake for irrigation of thirsty farmland. Both water bodies are open for fishing year-round and support significant game fish populations, including rainbow trout, bass, kokanee and walleye.

Much of the north central part of the Columbia Basin lies within the Channeled Scablands created by a series of Ice Age floods, mostly from Glacial Lake Missoula. Today this region shows a paucity of surface water. The largest inland water body is Moses Lake. Nearby Soap Lake is one example of a natural lake with high levels of minerals that fish cannot tolerate. Many other lakes and ponds in the mid-Columbia region today are man-made or created from seepage of irrigation diversion systems, including the Columbia Basin Irrigation Project. Examples of interior lakes with diverse fish populations include the Potholes Reservoir, Scootenay Reservoir, Dry Falls and Lake Lenore, among others. Small storage and flood control reservoirs in northeastern Oregon adjacent to the Columbia River with significant fish populations include Willow Creek, McKay and Cold Springs.

Inland lakes of the Columbia Basin are typically managed as mixed fisheries. Most are abundant with warmwater game fish such as yellow perch, largemouth bass, white crappie and bullhead catfish. Many also contain "rough" fish populations of carp, northern pikeminnow, tench, redside shiner and suckers. Some involve early-season, "put-and-take" fisheries for stocked rainbow trout. Backwaters, sloughs and small ponds are also common along the Columbia and Snake rivers. Most provide suitable habitat for fishes.

In the middle of the Great Columbia Plain, the Hanford Reach is unique as having riverine characteristics similar to those found historically throughout the region. The Hanford Reach is 51 miles long and bounded by the Yakima River near Richland, Washington, and the Priest Rapids Dam at river mile 390. The reach includes tall bluffs, backwater sloughs, cobble islands, 60-foot-deep pools and swift currents (Figure 1.4). This stretch of river supports the largest run of fall Chinook salmon on the West Coast of North America and is home to 45 species of resident and anadromous fishes. It is one of the few areas upstream of Bonneville Dam with a viable population of white sturgeons.

Figure 1.4. White Bluffs region, Hanford Reach (author photo)

In 1980, Ben Franklin Dam was proposed for construction upstream of Richland. This dam would have inundated the Hanford Reach, the last remaining free-flowing (albeit highly regulated) section of the Columbia River in the continental United States. One reason Ben Franklin Dam was never built was that increased water-surface elevation could have increased the transport of hazardous chemicals from past nuclear operations from contaminated groundwater to the river. It is ironic that the Hanford Site nuclear legacy resulted in preservation of the Hanford Reach for future generations of boaters and sportsmen.

The Hanford Reach was established as a national monument in 2000 by proclamation of President William J. Clinton. The U.S. Fish and Wildlife Service currently manages the reach and most surrounding land under agreement with the U.S. Department of Energy. Future uses are currently being determined through a stakeholder involvement process.

Downstream of the Hanford Reach are a series of hydroelectric dams known as lower Columbia River projects: McNary, John Day, The Dalles and Bonneville. Behind each dam are several miles of reservoir. Several large tributary streams enter the lower Columbia River from the Oregon and Washington sides. Downstream of Bonneville Dam, where salt water mixes with freshwater, are fishes that require access to the Pacific Ocean. There are anadromous populations of salmon and steelhead, smelt or eulachon, and two species of sturgeons. The floodplains here are highly productive and thus serve as important nursery areas for juveniles of all species.

In the two centuries since initial colonization of the Columbia Basin by white settlers, area waterways have undergone drastic changes. River flows were altered and lakes have been created where water-use practices have been modified. These practices have affected fishes in a variety of ways. Let's examine some of the more significant changes, for looking back often provides a view of what the future might hold.

Human Development Activities

Exploitation of abundant natural resources took many forms in the mid-Columbia region. The British-controlled fur trade, beginning in the early 1800s in north-central Washington, impacted tributary streams of the Columbia and Snake rivers in ways that are still being debated. One impact affected nature's engineer, the beaver, and how its widespread removal, in turn, affected headwater trout populations due to loss of pools, down-cutting of streambeds and less stable flow.

Less subtle in terms of impact to rivers and streams was gold and silver mining beginning in the mid-19th century. Redirection of stream channels and dredging decimated fish populations, particularly in the upper Columbia River valley. Metal- and ore-processing chemicals that drained from mine tailings rendered many streams lifeless. These impacts are still evident in several interior tributary streams where productivity of fishes and aquatic insects is reduced from metal contamination.

Ranching and intensive farming were the next change following initial settlement. Many riparian ecosystems were negatively impacted from overgrazing from the 1860s to about 1910. Streams in the Yakima and Methow river basins of the eastern Cascades and John Day River in the Blue Mountains were severely affected. Subsequently, floodplains adjacent to river channels were developed to capture fertile farmland. Associated irrigation practices have reduced streamflow.

Timber harvest increased in importance in the 20th century. Impacts on native populations of salmon and steelhead from these activities included migration blockage, loss of vegetative cover, reduced instream flows, sedimentation and elevated temperature. While improved forestry management practices are now in effect, many headwater areas may never fully recover.

Transportation has also been a factor in the demise of area fish populations. Deep passageways were carved into the bottoms of the lower Columbia and Snake rivers so that barges could float wheat and apples to downstream markets. Highways and railways were constructed along scenic rivers. Their roadbeds confined river flow and blocked access of stream fishes to headwaters.

Perhaps the most significant impact to aquatic habitats in the Columbia Basin has been from hydroelectric development. The creation of large reservoirs increased channel width, decreased available shoreline, and reduced the amount of shallow-water rearing and feeding areas important to juvenile salmon and steelhead (Figure 1.5). Reservoirs also favor increased abundance of non-native predators such as bass, walleye and channel catfish.

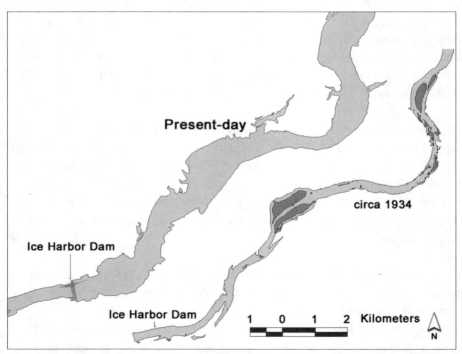

Figure 1.5. Plan form of lower Snake River (from D.D. Dauble et al. 2003, American Fisheries Society, Bethesda, Maryland)

In 1910, Swan Falls Dam eliminated nearly 25 percent of the upper Snake River available to migrating salmon and steelhead. The Hells Canyon complex, a series of three dams built from 1958 to 1967, blocked access to another 210 miles of the Snake River. Chief Joseph Dam blocked the upstream migration of Columbia River salmon at mile 545 in 1955. Overall, less than one-fifth of historic river features remain in the main stem Columbia River today because of hydropower development (Figure 1.6). Ironically, Bonneville Dam, completed in 1938, provided the first way for management agencies to accurately monitor the abundance of returning salmon and steelhead runs.

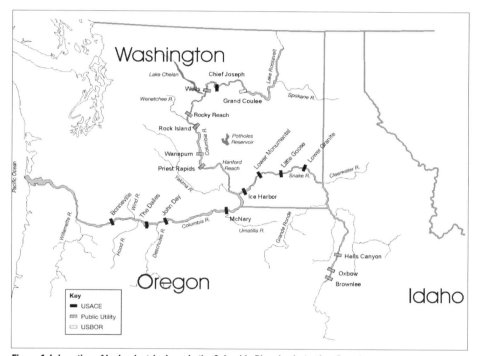

Figure 1.6. Location of hydroelectric dams in the Columbia River basin (author figure)

Grand Coulee Dam has a storage capacity of almost 10 million acre-feet. The 10 main stem dams in the Columbia River downstream of Grand Coulee are considered "run-of-river" with limited storage capacity. Flows in the Columbia River are now largely controlled by water released from storage reservoirs behind a series of high-head dams in Canada (Figure 1.7). In the Snake River, almost 25 percent of active water storage is diverted for irrigation, with the majority diverted in southern Idaho. The remaining water is released for power generation and other uses, including protection of migrating salmon and steelhead.

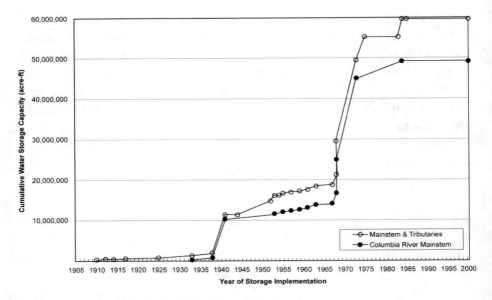

Figure 1.7. Storage capacity timeline for Columbia River (author figure)

So, what other changes from hydroelectric development affect fishes? First, upstream storage practices have reduced the size of the spring runoff. This means the large freshets that once scoured sediments and moved river gravel no longer occur. Operation of storage reservoirs has also reduced the average water velocity for, and the diversity of, habitat. Accumulated sediments require dredging for dams to operate as designed. The water level in reservoirs also changes hourly due to power-peaking practices, stranding small fishes along the shoreline and reducing productivity of nearshore regions. Finally, floodplain habitats have been lost in the lower Columbia River due to flow regulation.

It's not all about flow. Operation of main stem reservoirs has modified Columbia and Snake river water temperatures. Temperature extremes, or the range of annual change, have been moderated. In addition, reservoir operation has resulted in a "phase shift" where peak summer temperatures are delayed at least two weeks from the pattern observed historically. This change has altered upstream migration timing and behavior of adult salmon and steelhead. Interestingly, average water temperatures have not changed significantly, nor have maximum temperatures increased during this time period.

The impact of human development on water resources of the Columbia Basin has been extensive. It's hard to put a finger on any one thing because development activities are intertwined. One thing is sure: These changes have reduced the capacity of tributary streams to support populations of native salmon and steelhead and, in some cases, have led to increased abundance of non-native fishes such as bass and carp. The impact of harvest on fish populations is discussed in the next chapter.

• • •

"When spring and the salmon came, the Dreamer proclaimed that none could be eaten until the first roots were dug and the women could prepare a feast."

—Click Relander, *Drummers and Dreamers*, 1986

A Yakama Indian catches a king salmon on the Columbia River in Washington.

"Where have all the salmon gone? Were there no management programs to conserve the resource?"

—Courtland L. Smith, *Salmon Fishers of the Columbia*, 1979

Chapter 2. History of Fish Use in the Columbia Basin

At least 10,000 years before mountain men and intrepid explorers reached the Pacific Northwest, American Indian tribes were established throughout the region. Archaeological evidence indicates that American Indians fished from the earliest times until the present. After 1 A.D., evidence indicates that fishing increased dramatically, establishing the tools and techniques used by tribes prior to the arrival of explorers. For most American Indians, fish were one important part of a subsistence lifestyle.

This chapter begins with the role of fishes in tribal culture of recent millennia. Subsequent sections examine how 19th-century commercial harvest, followed by non-native species introductions, shaped fish populations of the Columbia Basin.

American Indian Lifestyles

The Columbia Plateau peoples lived a three-part economy, subsisting on roots, game or fish gathered during different parts of the year. Several tribes, including the Nez Perce, Wanapum and Umatilla, lived along the Mid-Columbia and lower Snake rivers, where they had ready access to abundant fisheries resources. The Wasco and Wishram Indians lived just east of the Cascade Mountains in Oregon and Washington and wintered close to the Columbia River. Increased mobility, after the horse was introduced to the region in the 1700s, expanded the range of native peoples previously relegated to fishing within or close to their own territory.

Chinook salmon were the most important species of fish for tribal fishers because of their abundance and because they could be harvested from spring through fall. Other fishes were important but available over shorter periods of time. Chinook salmon also had the widest distribution of the salmon, migrating from the Pacific Ocean to the headwaters of the Columbia and Snake rivers.

American Indian tribes established large fishing camps where the Columbia River narrowed and rapids were formed. These geological characteristics both funneled and concentrated upstream migrating salmon, thus increasing the odds of efficient harvest. The most productive fishing areas in the main stem Columbia River were at the Long Narrows (The Dalles), Celilo Falls and Kettle Falls. Other areas important to tribal fishers included P'na or Priest Rapids and Wy-Yow-Na near White Bluffs. Smaller fishing camps were established each summer just upstream of Wallula Gap and in the lower Snake River. Tribal fishing also occurred in most tributary streams where runs of anadromous salmon and steelhead were present. For example, a principal fishing place of the Priest Rapids Indians, known as Wan-a-wish, was near the present location of Horn Rapids Dam on the lower Yakima River. Here, tribal members gathered in the spring and early summer to catch Chinook salmon, blueback (sockeye salmon) and steelhead.

To the Wanapum Indians, or River People, the Columbia River was known as Nch'í Wána or "Big Water." The Wanapums, along with other American Indian tribes of the Pacific Northwest, had cultures deeply intertwined with fish and fishing. They were versatile with their choice of gear and resourceful in exploiting various species of fish.

The methods of 19th-century fishers are fascinating. At large rapids such as the "Long Narrows" of the Columbia River, Indians harvested returning adult salmon and steelhead from wooden platforms or rock ledges using long-handled dipping or scooping nets and gigs (Figure 2.1). At many historical fishing areas, adult salmon migrated upstream through narrow, basalt-lined passageways. These formations restricted movements and provided ample opportunity for fishing practices.

Figure 2.1. Wishram Indian spearing salmon (from Northwestern University Library, Edward S. Curtis' *The North American Indian: the Photographic Images*, 2001) http://memory.loc.gov/ammem/award98/ienhtml/curthome.html

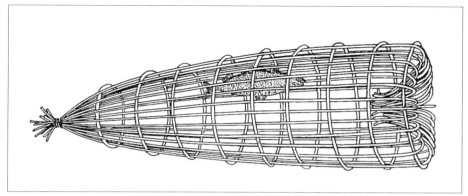

Figure 2.2. Fish weirs and traps constructed from willow branches (from D.E. Walker, Northwest Anthropological Research Notes, Inc., 1993)

In large rivers where the water was deep and currents swift, Indians fished at night in cedar canoes, using spears or gigs to catch salmon. Where there were sandy shoals, large seines (hauled nets) were a method of choice. Perforated and grooved stones were used as hook sinkers and anchor stones for gill nets and trotlines. In small tributary streams, they trapped "mullets" (sucker) and other resident fishes, such as cutthroat trout, with "hempen seines" or by using elaborate weirs and traps constructed from bent willow and rocks (Figure 2.2). Poison made from crushed nettle was used in limited situations to stun fish. Indian fishers also used their bare hands to collect salmon that were weakened after spawning.

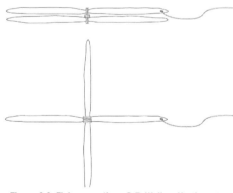

Figure 2.3. Fish gorge (from D.E. Walker, Northwest Anthropological Research Notes, Inc., 1993)

Fishing line was usually braided from native plants such as nettle and hemp. Early tribal anglers fashioned "gorges" from bone, wood or stone for use as hooks (Figure 2.3). Metal fishhooks and manufactured lines were later introduced by fur traders.

Arrival of the first salmon each year was an important event. At Kettle Falls, the "salmon chief" put his fishing basket or trap down before anyone else was allowed to start. When the first salmon appeared, they were to be roasted, not boiled. This custom was observed for several days. In some locations Indians did not catch fish until after they spawned because they were anxious to see the run continue. This approach to conservation ensured they would have a sufficient supply each year.

Indian fishing methods were designed to harvest large numbers of fish to be eaten fresh, traded or dried for later use. Salmon were split, backbone removed, sliced on each side and all parts preserved, including the head. Other body parts were favored at times. For example, the naturalist John Townsend noted Indian women "making breakfast of the great red salmon eggs."

American Indian tribes prepared salmon for storage over the winter by drying it in the sun or over a fire, pounding it and then layering it in baskets of woven grass and rushes. Each family might put away as much as 100 pounds of dried fish each fall. Dried salmon was packed into large bundles to be hidden underground among the rocks in secret caches for winter storage. Pounded fish or pemmican could be preserved this way for several years. At Palus, a large Indian village at the mouth of the Palouse River, Lewis and Clark noted the practice of digging holes in the riverbank to store dried fish. These pits served as natural refrigerators.

Although salmon accounted for a major part of the diet for the three- to six-month interval when they were available, many other fishes were important to American Indian tribes of the Columbia Basin. The Pacific lamprey or "eel" were much sought after as food when they were available. The Wanapum Indians had a well-known lamprey fishery near Pasco, Washington, a location referred to as Kosith, or "at the point of land." At this location, adult lamprey were caught at night from canoes with dip nets made of hemp. In locations such as Celilo and Kettle Falls, lampreys were snagged or gaffed off rocks where they attached to rest. Eugene Hunn, professor of anthropology at University of Washington in Seattle, writes about the Sahaptins intercepting a spawning run of "eels" during a root-gathering excursion up the North Fork, John Day River.

Pacific lamprey were boiled and slit open before grilling or dried over the fire and eaten like jerky. Nez Perce lore tells of medicine women collecting dripping fat from lamprey as they cooked over a fire. The oil was used in lamps and for medicines. Lampreys were preserved for later use in a manner similar to salmon.

Eulachon, or candlefish, were highly prized by lower Columbia River tribes and extensively traded with others. Alexander Ross, an early explorer to the region, wrote of how eulachon were sold by the fathom (6 feet) when laid head-to-tail. Indians dried eulachon by running a stick through their gills and hanging them in the smoke of lodges or over a small fire. A cloth or rush wick was placed down the mouth so they could be lit like a candle. Trails used by Indians where oil was carried for trade were known as "grease" trails. The hollow stem of kelp was a unique method used by coastal tribes to store and transport eulachon oil.

Curiously, sturgeons were not considered as food by all American Indian tribes. Sturgeons were sometimes disdained by the Sahaptin peoples of the Mid-Columbia who thought they interfered with salmon harvesting.

Some inland tribes referred to sturgeon as the "swallowing-monster's pet," perhaps fearing they were man-eaters due to their large size. In contrast, white sturgeons were important food fish for lower Columbia River tribes and at Kettle Falls on the upper Columbia. One innovative harvest technique involved killing a mountain goat in the cliffs above the river, leaving it in the shallows as "bait" and spearing sturgeon that came to feed on the carcass (Figure 2.4).

Figure 2.4. Petroglyph from the northern Columbia Plateau region (from J.D. Keyser, *Indian Rock Art of the Columbia Plateau*, University of Washington Press, Seattle, 1992)

Sculpin, or "Indian doctor fish," had cultural importance. They were respected and feared by Sahaptin-speaking people of the Mid-Columbia because they influenced the weather or had powers of foresight (Figure 2.5). Myths of origin describing how the eel (lamprey) lost his bones and how the sucker got his bones are among other fish stories passed down by local tribes.

Figure 2.5. Sculpin or "Indian doctor fish" (from C.E. Bond, *Keys to Oregon Fishes*, Corvallis, Oregon, 1994)

Abundant resident fishes were not ignored by tribal fishers. Mountain whitefish were prized when they converged on gravel bars to spawn in December and January. Whitefish and burbot could be caught through the ice to supplement the American Indian diet in the winter. Chiselmouth and sucker were often the first fish available in early spring. Longhouse congregations from the lower Columbia River held feasts in February to feed on sucker that migrated into small tributaries to spawn. These migrations were important because they occurred at a time when winter provisions were low and the spring salmon run was still several weeks away. Even small fish like redside shiners were considered a delicacy.

Fish parts were used for purposes other than food: vertebrae for beads, scutes of sturgeon as decoration, and spines as awls or needles for leatherwork. Glue was reportedly made from salmon skin to attach deer-leg sinews to a bow. Fish oil was often used as skin and hair lotion or burned as torches.

Some historians speculate that, based on a population of 50,000 people and a consumption rate of one pound per day during the entire year, the annual salmon catch of Indians in the 18th century could have approached 18 million pounds per year. These harvest rates were not sustained. Decimation of the Indian population by disease and conflict with white settlers decreased tribal fishing intensity by the early 1800s.

As the number of white settlers began to grow, conflicts with local Indian tribes became more intense. The Whitman massacre of 1847 and battles at The Dalles were two consequences of encroachment of white settlers on local Indian tribes. Consequently, Washington Territory Governor Isaac Stevens met with tribes of the Columbia River Basin in 1855 and established reservations. While the treaty of 1855 provided for fishing in the "usual and accustomed places," the lifestyles of American Indian peoples were changed forever.

Early treaties allowed both Indians and white settlers to fish for salmon together. There were few conflicts because it was thought that the supply of salmon to the Columbia River was inexhaustible. Although the commercial fishing season for white settlers enacted seasonal closures beginning in 1890, Indians were allowed to fish the entire year.

During the first part of the 20th century, the commercial Indian fishery was primarily with dip nets. However, with completion of Grand Coulee Dam in 1940, the major dip net fishery at Kettle Falls was eliminated. Indian fishing activities at Celilo Falls, the only remaining large dip net fishery, were carefully documented in a study conducted before The Dalles Dam was constructed. At that time, fishing for salmon and steelhead was done from wooden scaffolds or platforms perched precariously on bedrock shorelines and islands (Figure 2.6).

Figure 2.6. Celilo Falls fishing involved dipping from wooden platforms that were attached to basalt formations (Northwestern Museum of Arts & Culture/Eastern Washington State Historical Society, Spokane, Washington, L95-66.1 Clarence Colby)

Conditions were so dangerous that fishers were roped to their platforms. In the 1940s Indians used cable cars to travel to and from the mainland to various islands where they fished. Fishing locations varied by season according to water level. Fishing was typically restricted to daytime because of limited fish migration at night. Fishers used long-handled dip nets, either stationary (set) or movable. Occasionally, the fishers used small wire baskets constructed of chicken wire in whitewater locations where fish tended to fall back due to a strong current.

On September 17, 1947, near the peak of the fall run of Chinook salmon, 119 movable and 93 set dip nets were in operation each day with an average of three or four Indians attending each net. Based somewhat on these numbers, the Washington Department of Fisheries and Oregon Fish Commission estimated that up to 36,000 Chinook salmon, at an average weight of 20 pounds, were landed daily by Indians at Celilo Falls. These catches occurred when salmon runs were declining rapidly. This fishery ended abruptly. Celilo Falls was inundated after water levels rose 110 feet when The Dalles Dam was completed in 1957.

In 1974, U.S. District Judge George Boldt ruled that American Indian tribes had the right to fish at their accustomed places and were entitled to a 50 percent share of the annual catch or harvestable run. Treaty tribes affected by this ruling include the Yakama Nation, Confederated Tribes of the Colville Reservation, Confederated Tribes of the Warm Springs Indians and the Nez Perce. All have access to fisheries resources within the Columbia Basin, including the Columbia and Snake rivers and major tributaries.

The primary tribal fishery today is a set net (gill net) fishery in the lower Columbia River. Traditional methods of dipnetting for adult salmon from wooden platforms are still employed in the lower canyon of the Klickitat River, Sherar's Falls on the Deschutes River, the lower Yakima River near Wanawish (Horn Rapids Dam) and immediately downstream of some lower Columbia River dams. A tribal commercial and subsistence harvest of white sturgeon also takes place in the Columbia River. Methods used include set nets, set lines and occasionally hook-and-line. The present-day lamprey fishery is mainly limited to Willamette Falls, although small tribal fisheries exist at Sherar's Falls on the Deschutes River, Fifteen Mile Creek near The Dalles and on the Klickitat River.

Salmon Mythology

The Plateau peoples have a large collection of spoken narratives that describe the deeds and misdeeds of mythic beings. Most of the mythic people have animal names. A Wishram tribal narrative relates how Coyote released fish from a pond created by a dam the Sisters made at Celilo Falls. As punishment, the Sisters (as swallows) were to signal the return of Chinook salmon each spring. Another story from the Nez Perce relates how the amorous Coyote travels upriver, leading salmon only into those streams whose communities give him a woman and suckers.

Commercial and Sport Harvest Practices

Early settlers to the Pacific Northwest soon saw commercial potential in the abundant runs of salmon and steelhead. During the late 19th century, the fishing industry used a wide range of gear to harvest salmon, including horse-driven seine (Figure 2.7), purse seine, gill net, traps and fish wheel.

Figure 2.7. Seining with horses (University of Washington Libraries Special Collection. John N. Cobb UW 17228)

Commercial canning of salmon in the lower Columbia River was well operational by the 1870s, mostly from the mouth of the Columbia River to Celilo Falls. Runs of salmon in the middle and upper Columbia River were considered to be of lower quality. However, because most spawning areas were in the upper part of the Columbia Basin, harvest of salmon in the lower river dramatically reduced upriver populations.

Previously used in shad fisheries on the East Coast of the United States, fish wheels were introduced to the Columbia River in 1879 (Figure 2.8). Twenty years later, 76 were in operation. Although fish wheels captured less than 10 percent of the total commercial harvest of Columbia River salmon, their use was more controversial than other methods because of their efficiency. The No. 5 fish wheel near The Dalles was famous for catching a record 209 tons of salmon in 1906. When salmon runs declined, Oregon outlawed fish wheels in 1927. Washington followed by banning all traps, fish wheels, set nets and dragnets in 1934.

Figure 2.8. Catamaran fish wheel from the lower Columbia River, 1890 (courtesy of Oregon Historical Society, Columbia Gorge Discovery Center OrHi 4176)

Extensive hatchery development practices were initiated in the 1890s to rebuild declining runs of spring Chinook salmon. In 1910, the Pacific Coast Hatcherymen's Association was formed. Many fisheries managers believed that high levels of salmon harvest could be maintained. John Crawford, superintendent of hatcheries for the state of Washington, was quoted in 1911 as saying "This year's run of salmon proves beyond a doubt that there is absolutely no real reason for the eventual depletion of the stream by overfishing or the advance of civilization." He couldn't have been further from the truth.

Harvest of Chinook salmon peaked in 1883 when more than 40 million pounds were landed. Chinook salmon harvest averaged about 26 million pounds per year from 1880 to 1930. Estimated catch declined to 17 million pounds per year from 1931 to 1958 and to 7 million pounds from 1948 to 1973 (Figure 2.9). Columbia River coho catch peaked in 1895 at about 6 million pounds, sockeye in 1889 at 4 million pounds and steelhead at 4.5 million pounds in 1892.

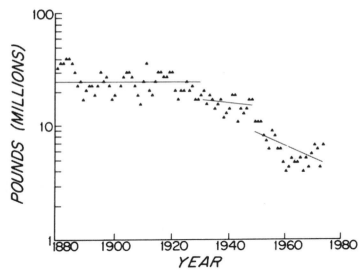

Figure 2.9. Commercial harvest for Chinook salmon in the Columbia River from 1880 to 1980 (modified from C.L. Smith, *Salmon Fishers of the Columbia*, Oregon State University Press, Corvallis, Oregon, 1979)

Not all commercial-fishing venues involved salmon. For example, in 1880, a white sturgeon fishery started in the lower Columbia River (Figure 2.10). Annual harvest reached a peak of 6 million pounds in 1892. The white sturgeon population was nearly decimated by 1899 because the take was primarily large brood stock. In the early days of the white sturgeon fishery, four products were taken: flesh, roe, spinal marrow or "bone," and the swim bladder or "sounds." Meat was eaten fresh, canned or smoked. Roe was processed for caviar, although the trade did not rival that of sturgeon from Asia-Europe. Bone was sold to Chinese and dried for use in soup. Sounds were used for manufacturing isinglass (a kind of gelatin used in making jellies), glue and for clearing ale.

From 1941 to 1949, there was a commercial lamprey fishery at Willamette Falls, near Oregon City. In 1946, a peak harvest of nearly 200 tons was taken to a reduction plant at Warrenton, Oregon. The fish were used primarily for vitamin oil and as protein in poultry and fish meal. The Oregon Department of Fish and Wildlife now issues permits for Indians and non-Indian subsistence use and for commercial fishing at Willamette Falls. Lampreys are collected there by hand with a limit of 100 per person. Annual commercial harvest since 1990 is about 10 tons. Presently, Pacific lampreys have value as a source of medicinal anticoagulants and fish bait.

Figure 2.10. Man on dock with sturgeon, circa 1900 (University of Washington Libraries Special Collection, John Fletcher Ford IND0635)

The total harvest of eulachon, or smelt, from the Columbia River and tributaries averaged about 2 million pounds per year from 1938 to 1994. A sharp decline in commercial harvest occurred in the mid-1990s. Smelt are harvested commercially by gill, trawl and dip nets in the main stem Columbia River downstream of Bonneville Dam and by dip nets in tributaries. The majority of the commercial catch occurs in the tributaries, with Cowlitz River landings leading the pack. The oil of smelt, which has the consistency of soft butter at room temperature, was once looked upon as a tonic substitute for cod liver oil.

The common carp also has a history of commercial fishing. Carp were brought to the Pacific Northwest in 1880 with intent to be grown in backyards, like poultry, but soon escaped to the lower Columbia River. A commercial fishery was developed where carp were sold for fertilizer at $5 per ton. In the 1930s, carp were sold at selected ethnic markets in Portland and Seattle for human consumption. There was also a flourishing commercial fishery for carp in Idaho from 1945 to 1965. The bulk of the harvest was sold to trout hatcheries or mink farms. Peak commercial harvest of carp in the Mid-Columbia region exceeded 1 million pounds per year during its heyday in 1969. Carp from Moses Lake, Banks Lake, Sprague Lake and the Columbia River near Pasco, Washington, were processed into dry meal and sold as fish meal. Current commercial harvest of carp, while regulated by state management agencies, is minimal.

The Columbia River Compact establishes commercial regulations for the Columbia River and tributaries. Within commercial catch limits are state regulations that designate sport regulations for harvesting and protecting fish populations. Recreational fishing regulations are established separately by management agencies of Oregon, Washington and Idaho. Restrictions may be placed on type of gear (e.g., artificial lures only), length of season and location. In some areas, only catch-and-release fishing is allowed.

There are two distinct commercial fisheries separated geographically by Bonneville Dam. Zones 1 through 5, downstream of Bonneville Dam, are open to all citizens. The treaty commercial fishery (also known as the Zone 6 fishery) extends upstream from Bonneville Dam to McNary Dam, except at the mouth of certain tributaries and adjacent to hatcheries. This treaty fishery is restricted to four Indian tribes (Nez Perce, Umatilla, Warm Springs and Yakama).

Sport fishing is an important use of the Columbia River today. Salmon, steelhead, sturgeon, smelt and shad are the principal sport fishes taken with salmon being the most important. Historically, Chinook salmon migrated upstream as a single run from March through October, with a peak in the summer (Figure 2.11). What is now termed summer-run Chinook salmon were referred to as "June Hogs" in the late 1800s because of their timing and large size. However, excess harvest reduced spring and summer runs of Chinook salmon to the point that both commercial and sport fishing had to be restricted. In the mid-1990s, the spring and summer runs rebounded to levels that allowed limited sport fishing opportunity. Greatest numbers of salmon were in the fall with the arrival of fall Chinook and coho salmon.

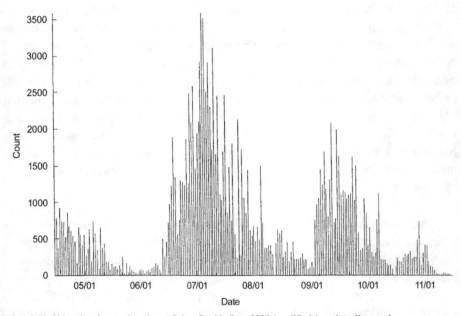

Figure 2.11. Chinook salmon migration at Priest Rapids Dam 2003 (modified from http://www.cbr.washington.edu, June 2007)

Most of the sport catch of upriver (summer) steelhead occurs in tributaries. Since 1984, sport regulations were enacted to protect wild summer steelhead. Only hatchery fish can be kept. Hatchery fish are identified by an adipose fin clip, although multiple fin clips are sometimes required before a steelhead can be harvested. The combined catch of Oregon, Washington and Idaho in the main stem Columbia and tributaries approached a peak of 100,000 steelhead in 1987.

Hatchery propagation and stocking of commercial and sport fishes was employed historically with intent to replenish economically important populations. Over the past century, fisheries managers have relied on hatcheries for all but a few species. Hatchery fish currently make up 80 percent of the salmon and steelhead returning to the Columbia River.

Rainbow trout are the most popular sport fish in cold-water tributaries and lakes of the region. Most stream-dwelling trout are native or self-sustaining populations, while the majority of lake and pond populations are stocked from state fish hatcheries. Brook trout and cutthroat trout also are planted in lakes of the Columbia Basin. It is not feasible to depend on natural production of trout to maintain populations in many lakes because suitable spawning areas are lacking.

A major consideration for current fisheries managers relates to regulatory protection of fishes listed for protection under the Endangered Species Act (ESA) of 1973, amended in 1978 and 1982. The ESA provides the authority for protection of threatened or endangered fish and their habitats. The U.S. Fish and Wildlife Service (USFWS) maintains the federal list of threatened and endangered species. The National Oceanic and Atmospheric Administration's (NOAA) National Marine Fisheries Service is responsible for the federal listing of anadromous fish. NOAA and USFWS also set policies for elements of the ESA, such as designating critical habitat for listed species.

Several steps are involved in protecting a fish stock listed under the ESA and for determining when it has recovered sufficiently to be taken off the list. Once a stock is listed, the federal action agencies produce a proposed action that describes what they will do to help protect it. They review the proposed action and issue a biological opinion on whether the proposed action will jeopardize the continued existence of the species. Recovery planning is the final step in the process. Hopefully, listed species and their ecosystems are restored and their future secured so that further protection under the ESA is unnecessary.

Table 2.1. Fishes currently protected under the Endangered Species Act that reside within the Columbia Basin.

NAME	LOCATION	STATUS
Chinook salmon	Snake River Fall run	Threatened
	Snake River Spring/Summer run	Threatened
	Upper Columbia River Spring run	Endangered
Steelhead	Snake River Basin	Threatened
	Lower/Middle Columbia River	Threatened
	Upper Columbia River	Endangered
Sockeye salmon	Snake River	Endangered
Chum salmon	Columbia River	Threatened
Bull trout	Columbia River system	Threatened
Oregon chub	Willamette River	Endangered

Introduction of Non-Native Fishes

As more and more settlers moved to the Pacific Northwest, they began to long for the white-meated pond fishes they were familiar with. Few native fishes of the region, except for salmon and trout, were deemed worthy of the frying pan. Immigrants were troubled that cane-pole fishes like bluegill and bass were not present. Catching a mess of catfish for a fish fry was also not possible. Consequently, homesick travelers came up with a plan. Why not import fishes they were familiar with? With the advent of rail, transporting fishes from the East Coast to the West Coast quickly became a possibility.

American shad were first to arrive on the scene. Shad were introduced to the Sacramento River in California in 1871. Introductions to the Columbia River followed, including a planting in 1886 near Wallula Junction, Washington. Catfishes were planted in lakes with outlets to the lower Columbia River in the early 1880s. Next came largemouth bass. Bass were introduced in Washington and Oregon lakes and the Boise River in the upper Snake River system in the 1890s. They were widely sold in markets from the beginning and not managed as a game fish until laws restricting such were enacted in 1913 and 1915.

Yellow perch also were brought to eastern Washington in 1890. Related species, including black crappie and bluegill, were reported in the Columbia River by 1903. These species were thought to originate from mixed plantings of adult bass and "other sunfish." Smallmouth bass were not widely introduced until 1923 to the Columbia Basin, where they quickly took hold. There was an exceptional fishery for smallmouth bass in the lower Yakima River as early as 1944. Walleye were introduced in the 1950s. These large predators were first stocked in Lake Roosevelt where they spread downstream through the Columbia River system. Walleye have since been planted in inland lakes where they are managed as part of a mixed fishery. Northern pike, introduced in the 1970s to northeastern Washington State, may expand their range to the Columbia River.

Warmwater fish species, or "spiny rays," are the fastest growing segment of the resident sport fishery in the Pacific Northwest. Over the past 40 years, the number of warmwater anglers has more than doubled in the state of Washington. Today, more than 60 percent of resident game fish sought by anglers are considered warmwater species. The most important species include bass, sunfishes, catfishes, yellow perch and walleye. In most situations, these popular "exotic" fishes reproduce successfully after being introduced.

Interestingly, leading fisheries scientists had little idea how species introductions would change aquatic ecosystems of the Columbia Basin. Introductions were made for more reasons than to provide sport fishing opportunity. Some were made to provide forage for desired predator species or biological control of unwanted insects and plants. Others occurred through accidental release, including bait and aquarium fishes. Of the 60 or so species of fishes present in the Columbia Basin today, only 30 are considered native. This only proves that we should be careful of what we long for. The implication of warmwater species introductions to native populations of fishes is discussed in more detail in chapter 4.

•••

"At about noon we struck the Walla Walla river, a very pretty stream of 50 or 60 yards in width, fringed with tall willows, and containing a number of salmon, which we can see frequently leaping from the water."

—John Kirk Townsend, *Narrative of a Journey*, September 2, 1834

Wallula Gap, Washington State Historical Society, Asahel Curtis 33541.

"Large collections of fishes were made at the various places where collecting was possible, and their study has greatly increased our knowledge of the variations in and the geographic distribution of the freshwater fishes of the northwestern United States."

—Charles H. Gilbert and Barton W. Evermann,
*A Report Upon Investigations in the Columbia River Basin,
With Descriptions of Four New Species of Fishes*, 1894

Chapter 3. Studies of Columbia Basin Fishes

When did the first studies of fishes occur in this region and how were they documented? To understand what fish were present in the Columbia Basin before oral history requires using the archaeological record. Some of the earliest evidence for aboriginal use of salmon has been found where major rapids and falls once were located. For example, salmon remains estimated at 8,000 years old have been found at The Dalles and at Kettle Falls, representing the upper and lower limits of the Columbia Basin. Remains of other common fishes, including sturgeons, suckers, minnows, three-spine sticklebacks and sand rollers also were found. At other sites, fish-related tools, including net weights, gorges and "fish walls" provided evidence of fishing.

Not until the 20th century were anthropologists able to reconstruct a list of fish species present in the Columbia River basin before white settlement. We know now that tribal fishers recognized six species of Pacific salmon and steelhead and distinguished among several species of resident fishes. In this regard, they were ahead of many 19th century scientists who managed to come up with a new species name for just about every variation in size and shape of new fish they encountered.

The Sahaptin-speaking people native to the Mid-Columbia Basin were well-acquainted with nearly all fish species in their waters because most were sought as food. The Sahaptin classification system included 20 kinds of fish that corresponded to about 30 species in ichthyology (Figure 3.1).

The grouping had close correspondence to current scientific nomenclature in both content and structure in that it was hierarchical and recognized two general categories of fishes. One category affiliated salmon and steelhead with lamprey and sturgeon (i.e., migratory species). The second category included resident fishes such as whitefishes, trout, suckers, minnows and sculpins. Although some species were closely aligned, others, such as sculpins and daces, were lumped into a single category of "residual small fish."

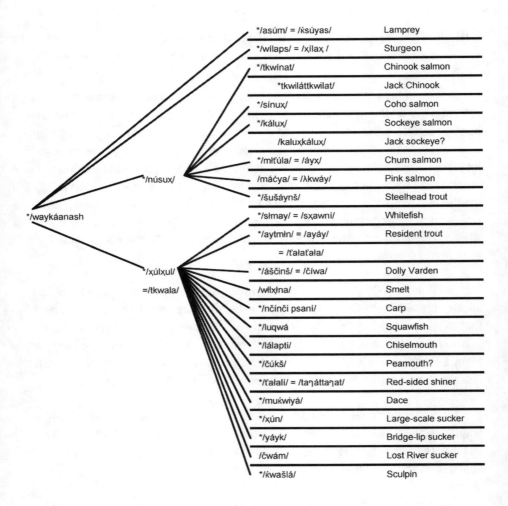

Figure 3.1. Fish taxonomy of the Sahaptin-speaking peoples (adapted from E.S. Hunn, Northwest Anthropological Research Notes, Inc. 1990)

Early Explorers to the Region (1805-1850)

The journals of Captains Meriwether Lewis and William Clark provide the first written documentation of fishes from the Columbia River system. Because neither explorer was trained in fish taxonomy, many of their accounts were inaccurate (note that editors of their journals were also inconsistent in interpretation). To round out his background, Lewis went to Philadelphia to learn about botany, zoology and Indian history with Dr. Benjamin Smith Barton. Barton taught Lewis how to preserve and label specimens and the Linnaean system for classifying specimens with two Latin names (i.e., the binomial method). Clark was the principal mapmaker and illustrator of journals of the expedition. He also sketched two fish species observed in the Columbia River: the "white salmon trout" (i.e., silver or coho salmon) and the eulachon or candlefish. We rely on anecdotal or written descriptions of all other species they encountered.

Captain Clark, upon his arrival to the mouth of the *Tape-tett* (Yakima River) on October 17, 1805, wrote, "The river is remarkably Clear and crowded with Salmon in maney (sic) places" (Figure 3.2). What Clark had witnessed was fall Chinook salmon migrating back to this productive confluence area to spawn. Members of the expedition had no knowledge of Pacific salmon life history, so they were perplexed as to why most salmon were dead or dying. One reason was that only one species of trout and salmon (then *Salmo*) previously had been described, from a Russian population, by Johann Walbaum in 1792. There were no previous collections from the United States.

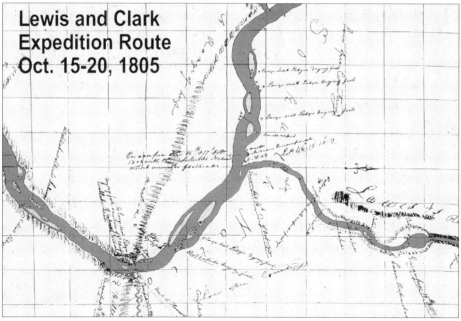

Figure 3.2. William Clark map of the confluence of the Snake and Columbia rivers, October 1805 (William Robertson Coe Collection, Yale University, New Haven, Connecticut)

Lewis and Clark's training was largely a crash course and limited in scope to knowledge that existed at that time. Neither explorer could spell well, as least by higher standards at the time. Names of plants and animals they encountered were spelled phonetically and capitalization was erratic. They often failed to recognize new species of fish, sometimes confusing them with those they were familiar with.

Two species of resident fish were mentioned by the expedition as it passed through the mid- and lower Columbia River. The first entry was on April 16, 1806: "At the rapids the natives subsist chiefly on a few white-salmon trout ... and considerable quantities of a small indifferent mullet of an inferior quality." Lewis and Clark again referred to mullets (i.e., suckers) when they were presented with a platter of "3 rosted (sic) mullets" by the Walla Walla tribe on their return upriver in 1807. Clark provided a detailed sketch of a fish weir and described seining methods that local Indians used to collect mullets from the lower Walla Walla River.

The other resident fish account was made by Lewis. He described how a small Indian boy "caught several chubbs with a bone (in this form) which he substituted for a hook" near the present location of Plymouth, Washington, at Wallula Gap. There was no mention of bait, which indicates the small gorge functioned as a lure. Descriptions from the journal entry suggest the fish was a peamouth chub. This fish was cited by Barton Evermann, an early taxonomist and fishery biologist, as one of the more abundant fish in the Mid-Columbia River region in the late 19th century.

During most of their journey, Lewis and Clark's party relied on Indian tribes encountered along the way for a fish dinner. It wasn't always salmon. Several journal entries in February and March 1806 described eulachon. Meriwether Lewis was most enamored with this small fish, finding it "more delicate and lussious (sic) than the white fish of the lakes." Joseph Whitehouse, another member of the party, wrote: "The small fish, which had the resemblance of a herring but much better tasted."

Sturgeon also found their way to the meal table. According to Lewis, sturgeon that had "been cut into large flatches" were laid on top of fire-heated stones, then layered with small boughs or leafy branches. Once all the meat was laid down, the stack was covered with mats and water was poured over it and among the hot stones. This process caused steam and cooked the fish in an hour or so. Patrick Gass, a member of the expedition, also made reference to sturgeon, "We passed several Indian lodges where the natives were fishing for sturgeon and got a large one out of a canoe."

Only one member of their party, Private Silas Goodrich, appeared to have an interest in fishing as a sport. Clark wrote in the early summer of 1805, "Goodrich who is remarkably fond of fishing caught several douzen (sic) fish of two species."

It also was reported the private favored use of bait over artificial lures; "They bite on meat and grasshoppers." Later in the summer, his talents were alluded to again: "Goodrich who is our principal fisherman caught several fine trout." Goodrich's skills were apparently not translatable to salmon because journal entries alluded to the fact that salmon wouldn't take lures on at least two occasions.

Based on a review of journal entries, Lewis and Clark and other members of the expedition encountered up to 11 species of fish west of the Continental Divide (Table 3.1). However, Lewis noted (March 2, 1806), "I have no doubt there are many other species of fish, which also exist in this quarter of different seasons of the year, which we have not had the opportunity of seeing."

Table 3.1. List of fishes collected by Lewis and Clark while the expedition was in the Columbia Basin during 1805 and 1806, including current nomenclature.

Lewis & Clark	Common Name	Scientific Name
Salmon	Chinook or king salmon	*Oncorhynchus tshawytscha*
Red char	sockeye or blueback salmon	*O. nerka*
White salmon	coho or silver salmon	*O. kisutch*
Speckled trout	cutthroat trout*	*O. clarki*
Salmon trout	steelhead (adult form)	*O. mykiss*
Trout	rainbow trout	*O. mykiss*
Chubb (sic)	peamouth	*Mylocheilus caurinus*
Mullet	largescale sucker	*Catostomus macrocheilus*
Eulachon or Ulken	candlefish or smelt	*Thaleichthys pacificus*
Sturgeon	white sturgeon	*Acipenser transmontanus*
Bottlenose	mountain whitefish*	*Prosopium williamsoni*

* Likely present but not documented by the expedition west of the Continental Divide

The Canadian explorer David Thompson was next to arrive on the scene. Thompson provided several accounts of fishes from the Columbia Plateau during his travels from 1807 to 1812. Thompson reported 20 families fishing for salmon near the confluence of the Snake and Columbia rivers. In another journal passage, he described obtaining a 52-inch-long Chinook salmon from a local Indian tribe. This specimen must have weighed more than 60 pounds.

Because Thompson was not a trained naturalist, his naming of fishes was muddled. For example, he frequently interchanged the terms "carp" and "mullet" with sucker. He also referred to mountain whitefish as "herring." These common names were familiar to him but were incorrect when applied to Pacific Northwest fishes present at the time.

Curiously, Thompson used the terms "salmon" and "small salmon" throughout his journals. "Salmon" were most likely Chinook salmon. I believe he used the term "small salmon" when he encountered jack Chinook salmon (a precocial or early-maturing male), based on run timing and because Sahaptin taxonomy, with which he was familiar, considered jack salmon as "little Chinook salmon."

To his credit, Thompson noted six different species of salmon and steelhead, similar to local Indian tribes. In contrast to Lewis and Clark, he was aware that salmon died after spawning: "It is the popular belief that all Salmon that enter the River die and no one ever returns." Thompson also advanced the state of knowledge by documenting that salmon returned to their home stream each year to spawn: "No two species enters the same stream to spawn, and that each species enters a separate River for the purpose." Unfortunately, his thoughts on use of separate streams during spawning were not entirely correct. Many salmon populations share the same river system.

Alexander Ross was next, passing through the Mid-Columbia right on David Thompson's heels. Ross encountered a group of Indians from the local Walla Walla tribe who may have participated in an early precursor to fly fishing. The scene played out near the midpoint of Ross' 600-mile canoe trip from Fort Astoria to an outpost near the Okanogan River in September 1811. Ross put ashore at daylight just upstream of the Yakima River when four Indians on horseback joined his party. One Indian cut a small patch of leather from his shirt "about the size of a small bean." He tied the piece of leather to a section of line braided from horsehair, "entered the river a little way, sat down on a stone," and proceeded to catch several small fish 3 to 4 inches long. Ross went on to further describe this novel form of fishing. "When the fish got hold of the bit of wet leather ... their teeth got entangled in it, so as to give time to jerk them to shore." So, what were these small fishes? Among fishes present in the Mid-Columbia River then, only a few are known to strike an artificial lure. Of these, only salmon and trout have sharp teeth in their mouth. Given this clue, the time of the year and relative abundance, there's a good chance that the mystery breakfast fare involved juvenile Chinook salmon.

The journals of Alexander Ross show the importance of tools made of steel as barter with local tribes: "A needle was given for a salmon, an awl for ten, and a knife for fifty!" Evidently, salmon were much easier to come by than a good knife.

Ross also mentioned that the Snake River was warmer and more turbid than the Columbia River. From his entry of August 15, 1811, we learn, "At the junction of the waters, Lewis's River has a muddy or milk-and-water appearance and is warm; while the Clarke's River is blueish, clear, and very cold." Interestingly, temperatures in the lower Snake River remain higher than the Columbia River today.

Some early explorers referred to salmon in less positive terms. For example, Gabriel Franchere, traveling upriver from Fort George in 1814, wrote that salmon were a dietary challenge for some due to their high oil content, "a fact that makes it unwholesome for those who are not accustomed to it and eat large amounts." Wild raspberries served as a remedy for the diarrhea that often followed such a meal.

Other naturalists continued to provide anecdotal information on local fishes and Native American fishing practices. For example, John Kirk Townsend reported July 3, 1835, that Indians were taking "thousands" of lamprey eel at a location somewhere between The Dalles and the Utalla (Umatilla) River; "They are seen hanging in great numbers in their lodges to dry in the smoke." (Figure 3.3) Another of his journal entries described that Indians prefer to fish in "slues" and creeks rather than the "big river." Townsend's greatest contribution to natural history of the Pacific Northwest was detailed observation of birds of the region. Appropriately, his legacy is the Townsend's solitaire, a thrush of Western mountain forests.

Figure 3.3. Camp of Billy Barnhart on the banks of the Umatilla River c. 1903 showing "eels" or Pacific lamprey drying on a rack (Special Collections & University Archives. University of Oregon Libraries. ORU_PH036_5609)

The traveling artist, Paul Kane, captured American Indian lifestyles in several paintings during his travels in the 1840s (Figure 3.4). From July to September 1847, he roamed the Mid-Columbia region where "the Walla Walla River debouches into the Columbia River" and near the "Paluce or Pavilion River" (Palouse). His journals include tales of rattlesnakes, Indian lore and salmon fishing. He also speculated about effects of windblown sand on the dental health of the Walla Walla tribe! "The salmon, while in the process of drying, also become filled with sand to such an extent to wear away the teeth of the Indians."

Figure 3.4. Paul Kane (1810–1871), *Drying Salmon*, watercolor and pencil on paper, 5-1/2 x 9-5/16 inches (14.0 x 23.6 cm), Stark Museum of Art, Orange, Texas, 31.78/50, WWC 50

Perhaps Kane's greatest contribution to our understanding of Columbia River fishes occurred while he was at Fort Colville. Here Kane documented the timing and abundance of the salmon run at Kettle Falls along with other details on Indian fishing practices. For example, he wrote that salmon first arrived in mid-July and that they ascended the falls for nearly two months: "In fact there is one continuous body of them, more resembling a flock of birds than anything else in their extraordinary leap up the falls." Kane also provided an early reference to angling for salmon: "No angler, although frequent trials have been made by the most expert in the art, has yet succeeded in tempting them to take any description of fly or other bait." Wouldn't he be surprised to see how far sport fishing methods have evolved in pursuit of salmon today!

First Scientific Expeditions (1840-1900)

The first comprehensive study of the Columbia Basin was the U.S. Exploring Expedition. In 1841, Lieutenant Charles Wilkes sent a party inland to the Hudson Bay post at Fort Colville, passing near the junction of the Snake and Columbia rivers. Two years later, John C. Frémont led an overland expedition of emigrants across the Rocky Mountains to Fort Vancouver. His guides included the mountain man Tom "Broken Hand" Fitzpatrick and the frontiersman Kit Carson. Frémont developed detailed maps of the Oregon trails, complete with locations of river crossings, grazing land and Indian tribes.

Although both expeditions were instructed to report on plants and animals of the region, little information on natural history of this region resulted. Louis Agassiz, a renowned Swiss scientist with major works on fishes of central Europe and Brazil, was selected to describe and publish on the fishes of the Exploring Expedition. His publication *Ichthyological Fauna of the Pacific Slope of North America* included detailed descriptions of Columbia River minnows: chiselmouth, squawfish (northern pikeminnow) and peamouth.

By 1850, the discovery of gold in California further stimulated the interest of westward travel. However, the only way to get to the Pacific Coast from the East Coast was either by ship around Cape Horn or by horse and wagon over hundreds of miles of desert, plains and mountains. To resolve this problem, the U.S. government sponsored another series of expeditions designed to gather information on new territory in western North America.

What followed in 1853 was the Topographical Corps, which conducted a series of surveys across the West to determine the most feasible route for a transcontinental railroad. The northern survey occurred between the 47th and 49th parallels and was led by Isaac I. Stevens, governor of Washington Territory. From 1857 to 1861, the Northwest Boundary Surveys were undertaken to characterize the 409-mile northwestern boundary between American and British territory. The focus was related to "species thought to yield the greatest economic benefit to the region." Thus, the distribution and abundance of salmon and steelhead populations was examined.

An eager team of naturalists accompanied all expeditions. One outcome was several scientific papers describing "new" species of salmon and trout. Three of the 13-volume series from the Pacific Railroad Report were devoted to zoological findings. The series included four monographs, one each for mammals, birds, reptiles and fishes. Charles Girard, the Smithsonian's first ichthyologist, did the report on fishes. Based on current taxonomy, his descriptions included seven different species of salmon and trout.

George Suckley, physician and naturalist, also reported on fishes of the Pacific Railroad Surveys. In addition, Suckley wrote on new species of *Salmonidae* collected during the Northwest Boundary Survey. His book, published posthumously in 1874, *On the North American Species of Salmon and Trout*, was overly generous in terms of 43 species described. However, according to Spencer Baird, then director of the U.S. National Museum and Commissioner of Fish and Fisheries, the publication "will serve as an excellent basis for further investigation."

The 70-page monograph on salmon and trout also provided early documentation of sport fishing methods of Western streams. Fly fishing for trout in streams near Fort Dalles was said to be good from April through July when "fish themselves are active, plump, and delicious, affording good sport." Other passages admitted to the practice of fishing with salmon-roe, meat or grasshoppers. A most unique bait was the meat of a crow: "This flesh combines redness and a rank smell with its proverbial toughness – all important desiderata."

In 1880, David Starr Jordan, the most influential of all American ichthyologists, was asked by Spencer Baird, secretary of the Smithsonian, to survey fishes of the Pacific Coast. Subsequently, Jordan and his assistants collected fishes along the entire West Coast, from Mexico to Canada. Jordan's various expeditions complemented the railroad and boundary surveys and formed much of the basis for the classic *Fishes of North and Middle America*, published in 1900.

In 1892, ichthyologists Charles Gilbert and Barton Evermann made large collections of fishes in the Columbia Basin, chiefly for the purpose of selecting a site for a salmon hatchery (Figures 3.5 and 3.6). Included in their reports were first-time descriptions of several species of minnow and sculpin. Other fishes observed included sand roller, sucker, dace, redside shiner, mountain whitefish, bull trout, white sturgeon, "three-toothed" (Pacific) lamprey, and the "squaremouth" (chiselmouth).

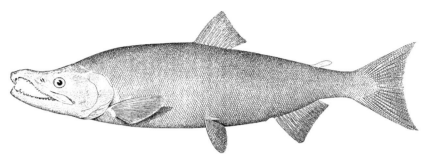

Figure 3.5. Adult redfish (sockeye salmon) from the upper Snake River (from B.W. Evermann, *A Report upon Salmon Investigations in the Headwaters of the Columbia River, in the State of Idaho, in 1895*. U.S. Government Printing Office, Washington, 1896)

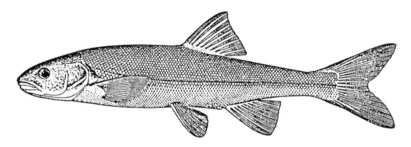

Figure 3.6. Peamouth chub from the Willamette River (from B.W. Evermann and S.E. Meek, *A Report upon Salmon Investigations in the Columbia River Basin and Elsewhere on the Pacific Coast in 1896*. Bulletin of the United States Fish Commission, 1897)

Despite the best efforts of several outstanding ichthyologists, the taxonomy of 19th century salmon and trout was confusing to say the least. Perhaps it was best summed up by the words of Elliot Couse who expounded in a footnote to the 1904 edition of Volume II of *History of the Expedition under the Command of Lewis and Clark*: "A pernicious activity of various misguided ichthyologists has resulted in making more than 30 nominal species of several baseless genera, of Pacific Coast *salmonidae*, all but five species of one genus of which are now allowed by judicious naturalists to lapse into innocuous desuetude, as the alleged specific characters have proved to be simply variations due to sex, age, seasons, and the fresh or spent condition of the fish." Amen.

Early taxonomic confusion resulted in part from poor preservation methods. It wasn't until the end of the 19th century before fish were preserved in formaldehyde and taken back to museums for detailed examination and measurement. Even then, field studies were limited to sampling fishes in their natural setting. Studies of life history and habitats were not undertaken until later. We now know that a thorough understanding of fish habits at different life stages is integral to having correct species identification.

Modern Fisheries Science

Ichthyologists of the early 20th century furthered the growing tradition of natural history or observational science. Consequently, early scientific publications often included detailed drawings of fishes in a natural setting. They also tended toward anthropomorphic explanations of fish behavior. One example was University of Washington ichthyologist Leonard Schultz's description of the spawning habits of peamouth chub. Schultz describes, "At times half a dozen or more females were pursued by numerous groups of males, a few of these often coming into a crowded group of males, whereupon much activity and splashing took place, sufficiently strong to splash water on my shoes, one and a half feet away." Behavioral descriptions of this type are rarely found in modern fishery journals. A well-thought-out experimental approach having robust statistical rigor is the current benchmark of fisheries science.

It wasn't until 1936 when Schultz and fellow University of Washington ichthyologist, Allan DeLacy, created the first comprehensive catalog of fishes from the states of Washington and Oregon. Their list of fish species and distribution was compiled from published records, specimens collected by ichthyologist Carl L. Hubbs, Schultz and students at the University of Washington. This scholarly contribution to fishes of the region serves as a valuable reference today.

Around this time, the U.S. Fish and Wildlife Service (then the Bureau of Fisheries) began studies to provide information needed to maintain and restore the fisheries of the Columbia River. Their focus was on migrating or anadromous species, especially salmon and steelhead. One study involved detailed surveys of all the streams of the Columbia Basin that "provide, or provided in the past, suitable spawning and rearing habitat." Data were collected on obstacles to migration, the species and numbers of fish inhabiting various tributaries, sources of pollution, water temperature and flows. The results of these decade-long studies were published in a series of special scientific reports in 1950.

With the period of intensive hydroelectric development came a slew of studies to identify important production areas used by salmon and steelhead. A misguided presumption was that future losses of anadromous salmonids could be mitigated with either artificial production or relocation of natural spawning populations. L.A. Fulton, a U.S. Fish and Wildlife Service biologist, summarized pertinent information on populations of steelhead, Chinook, coho, sockeye and chum salmon in the Columbia River Basin in the 1960s. Fulton's works are still used for restoration planning.

The past 50 years of research has resulted in hundreds of scientific reports on fishes. Many were funded by agencies responsible for the mitigation of fisheries resources impacted by the construction and operation of the Columbia Basin hydrosystem. These "action agencies," as they are sometimes known, include the U.S. Army Corps of Engineers, Bonneville Power Administration and U.S. Bureau of Reclamation. For the most part, current funding emphasizes fishes deemed important to sport and commercial interests, with emphasis on species listed for protection under the Endangered Species Act.

Several exceptions to salmon-centric studies have occurred in the Columbia River Basin during the past three decades. From 1973 to 1982, a series of studies on fishes of the Hanford Reach were conducted prior to planned siting of Washington Nuclear Projects 1 and 4. A total of 44 species were described, contributing much of the information described in this book. In the 1980s, University of Idaho personnel conducted extensive surveys of resident and anadromous fishes inhabiting the four lower Snake River reservoirs to evaluate the impact of dredging and sediment disposal. They identified a rich assemblage of native and introduced species. In the 1990s, the Washington Department of Fish and Wildlife and the U.S. Geological Survey surveyed predator fish populations in Mid-Columbia reservoirs. Limited studies of resident fish communities also were conducted in the past decade as part of Federal Energy Regulatory Commission re-licensing activities at Mid-Columbia dams. Minnows and suckers were generally the most abundant of the 38 species of fishes collected. Concern about water quality conditions of the lower Columbia River and streams in the Willamette River Basin resulted in extensive fish sampling in the 1990s as part of the National Water-Quality Assessment Program of the U.S. Geological Survey. Recent interest in warmwater fishes has spurred population surveys of interior lakes of the Columbia Basin by fisheries managers of the states of Washington and Oregon.

•••

"Fishes have more senses than ourselves."
 —Q. Bone and N.B. Marshall, *Biology of Fishes*, 1982

Fish ladder on the Walla Walla River on the edge of Milton-Freewater in eastern Oregon

"Knowledge of the behavior of an animal is essential to understanding of how changes in the environment influence its distribution and abundance."
 —C.E. Warren, *Biology and Water Pollution Control*, 1971

Chapter 4. Ecology and Behavior of Fishes

Ecology is the study of how plants and animals relate to one another. The word ecology is derived from the Greek term *oikos*, which means "house." Extending the concept to fishes requires studying the relationship among fishes and other members of aquatic ecosystems. Understanding the importance of these relationships involves knowing what fishes feed on, habitats they select and how they interact with other fishes.

One way to understand the role of a fish in the environment is to look at its stomach contents. Seeing what the fish I caught had eaten fascinated my children. They clustered around the kitchen sink and marveled at what came out of each fish's stomach. Most fishermen examine the stomach contents of their catch to figure out what it's eating. Casual observation is another technique. Try sitting on a stream bank to watch feeding behaviors. Whether trout sip, swirl or splash provides information on the type and life stage of insect they feed on. Fly fishermen apply this knowledge to more effectively "match the hatch."

Studies of fish ecology typically focus on a species' life histories and their environmental requirements. By life history, I mean the way a fish lives or carries out its life cycle, including how and where it lives. Before discussing life history requirements of fishes, some knowledge of the structure and function of aquatic ecosystems is warranted.

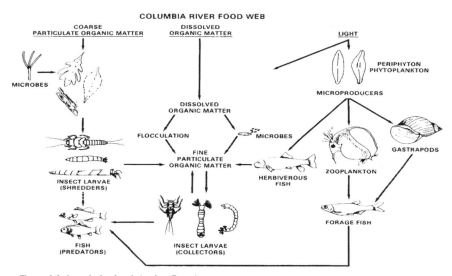

Figure 4.1. Aquatic food web (author figure)

Aquatic Food Webs

In aquatic ecosystems, microscopic plants or algae are the starting point for food webs (Figure 4.1). Algae convert the sun's energy into new organic matter through photosynthesis in a process known as primary production. Attached algae (periphyton) contribute most of the primary production in streams and rivers of the Columbia Basin while suspended algae (phytoplankton) predominate in reservoirs and lakes.

Most algae on river rock are diatoms (Figure 4.2). The German word *aufwuchs* is used to describe the complex matrix of algae, bacteria and microscopic animals on the surface of river rock. This film layer makes treacherous conditions when wading along the shoreline in the summer. Its pronunciation has nothing to do with what one might say after slipping and falling on one's backside.

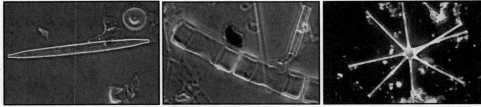

Figure 4.2. Columbia River diatoms (photos by William Hanf)

Algae are consumed by zooplankton, microscopic animals that live in the water column, and aquatic insects – the next level of the aquatic food web. Several species of fish also consume algae. Have you ever seen light-colored scrape marks on rocks that become exposed at low river flow? These thumbnail-sized marks appear where bottom-feeding fish like sucker and chiselmouth scrape the velvet-like layer of algae from river rocks (Figure 4.3).

Figure 4.3. Scrape marks left on river cobble (author photo)

Larger aquatic plants or macrophytes are important to aquatic ecosystems because they provide both food and cover for fishes. The depth and distribution of aquatic plants depend on the depth that light penetrates (photic zone). In large rivers, rooted aquatic plants are limited to backwater or shoreline areas of low velocity where sediments accumulate. Emergent plants, including cattail and bulrush, grow along the shoreline of ponds and lakes of the Columbia Basin. Submerged plants may be found in deeper water. Curled-leaf pond weed and introduced Eurasian water milfoil are common in lakes and ponds. Shallow water areas with abundant vegetation are highly productive for fishes because of the high densities of insects and zooplankton found there.

Small rivers of the Mid-Columbia have little rooted submerged vegetation except in lower reaches where sediment has built up. Cover for fishes is largely in the form of overhanging alder. Side channels may have duckweed (*Lemna*) and frog's bit (*Elodea*).

The boundary between water and land, often a matrix of alder, willow or bulrush, can provide subtle connections. Imagine a western kingbird hovering to feed on an emergent caddisfly that recently transformed from larvae living on the creek bottom. As if payback is required, a hungry trout lurking behind a root wad grabs a beetle falling from an overhanging branch. Nature is dynamic in this way.

Almost all fishes eat aquatic insects at some point in their life cycle. Caddisflies are perhaps the most visible and abundant of all insects within Mid-Columbia streams. If you wade in the shallows of most streams flowing from the Blue Mountains, you will see pebbly cases lined up on the top of rocks like single-wide trailers in a mobile home park. A unique species of caddisflies from the Hanford Reach of the Columbia River spins a net for gathering detritus from the drift. The adult form looks like a small, brown moth. When caddisflies emerge in the summer, they form dense clouds that congregate near shoreline willows. Other common aquatic insects that fish feed on include midge flies, stoneflies and mayflies. The latter two types are more common in tributary streams. Dragonflies and damselflies are abundant in lakes and ponds of the region. Fishes are attracted to larval, nymph and adult life stages of insects.

Crayfish or "freshwater lobster" are large, mobile invertebrates found in local waterways. Because of their size, they are important food for large predatory fish such as northern pikeminnow and bass. Other invertebrates include mussels and clams that filter dissolved and particulate matter from the water. Native mussels are becoming more rare in the Mid-Columbia and other parts of the United States because of changes to flow, temperature and water quality. The "floater" is a mobile, ridge-backed clam that can grow to 6 inches in length. It leaves a narrow trail in the mud when using its pseudopodia, or soft muscular foot, to push along the bottom. The Asiatic clam *Corbicula* was introduced to the Pacific Northwest by Chinese immigrants in the late 19th century. This highly invasive, yellow-brown clam lines irrigation canals and the shores of the Columbia and Snake rivers. Snails and limpets provide limited food value for bottom-feeding fishes like carp, sucker and white sturgeon.

Aquatic food webs are the basis of how plants and animals interact with one another in lakes and streams of the Columbia Basin. Fish, at the top of the food web, depend on the dynamics of aquatic ecosystems. Understanding life history requirements of fishes provides important clues about their behaviors. The following section focuses on specific behaviors that influence the distribution and abundance of fishes in regional waterways.

Life History Strategies of Fishes

Primary life history strategies of fishes relate to spawning and reproduction, feeding and migration. Without exception, behavior associated with these life-cycle events is designed to increase their chance of survival.

Spawning and Reproduction

Most fishes in Columbia Basin waterways take no care of their eggs after they spawn. They broadcast large numbers of eggs over the bottom substrate or among aquatic vegetation. Such fishes include yellow perch, walleye, carp, redside shiners, northern pikeminnow and suckers. After eggs hatch, developing larvae remain on the stream bottom, hidden within the substrate or within the vegetation, until they get bold enough to feed.

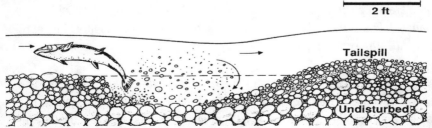

Figure 4.4. Salmon and steelhead deposit eggs in redds constructed by excavating river gravel and cobble with their tail (author figure)

Other fishes build nests to increase survival during the critical incubation and hatching stage. Salmon and trout construct nests (redds) by digging a depression in the gravel bottom of rivers with their tails (Figure 4.4). Following spawning, the female covers up the eggs with gravel and guards her redd for one to two weeks. Scientists monitor salmon spawning in the Hanford Reach of the Columbia River annually by aerial surveys. Salmon redds are highly visible from the air due to high water clarity (Figure 4.5). Eggs of Chinook salmon remain well-protected in the redd while alevins develop over the winter. Closely related species, such as mountain whitefish, may not prepare nests for spawning.

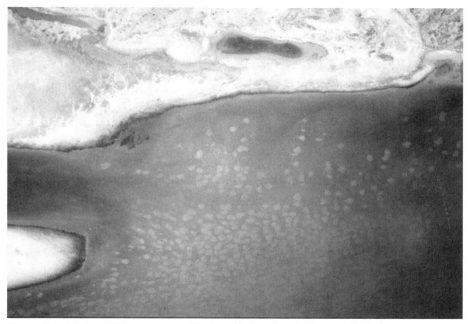

Figure 4.5. Aerial view of Chinook salmon redds (from U.S. Department of Energy collection)

Nests of other fishes vary widely in size, shape and material. For example, three-spine sticklebacks make a hollow nest from debris glued together with a sticky kidney secretion that the male excretes. Channel catfish and bullheads build nests by burrowing in a sloping bank or make shallow nests in mud and sand bottom, usually near cover such as submerged logs or among roots of aquatic vegetation.

Members of the sunfish family clear a circular depression on gravel or sand bottom. Female sculpins deposit clusters of adhesive eggs to the underside of a boulder or a flat rock that are then guarded by a male. A common element of nest-building strategies is protection of vulnerable eggs and embryos from predators.

Feeding

The overall food demand of fish is a function of their metabolic rate. Ultimately, a fish's body size, water temperature and activity affect the amount of food it requires to grow and reproduce. This relationship means a largemouth bass cruising around in warm water requires more food to sustain itself than does a sedentary channel catfish living under the ice. Thus, use of stealth or camouflage behavior to obtain food may be favored over constant swimming.

Fish species are often grouped into categories related to their feeding habits. This leads to terms like "bottom-feeders" and "predators." One group of bottom-feeders from the Columbia Basin includes suckers and chiselmouth that eat attached algae and other plant material. Predators are adult fish that eat insect larvae and smaller fish. Smallmouth bass, walleye and northern pikeminnow are in this category. Fish that prey entirely on other fish are called piscivores.

A large percentage of fish eat a wide range of food; that is, they are omnivores. In addition, all fish alter their diet as they grow. For example, fish larvae eat mainly microorganisms. As they grow, they switch to larger food items.

Knowing what fish eat can provide clues to their behavior. Sight feeders like rainbow trout hang out near current edges to grab insects that drift by. Suckers spend most of their time in shallow riffles where algae and other microorganisms they feed on thrive. Bass often lurk near cover to use a lay-and-wait strategy for grabbing small fishes. These associations are not random.

Feeding habits relate to the position and structure of a fish's mouth and its digestive tract. For example, fish with an inferior or down-turned mouth, such as suckers and dace, are well adapted to feed on the bottom of lakes and streams. Trout have a terminal mouth that allows them to feed anywhere in the water column. Fishes with an upturned mouth, e.g., mosquitofish, tend to be surface feeders.

Columbia Basin fishes exhibit large differences in mouth size and shape, as well as variations in the number, size and placement of teeth. Teeth may occur in the jaw, which walleye find useful for grabbing and tearing prey; in the tongue, which aids cutthroat trout in holding prey; or in the pharyngeal region that carp use for crushing clams and other hard-shelled animals. Filter-feeding fishes tend to have a large number of close-spaced gill rakers that strain microscopic plants and animals from the water column.

The internal organs, or guts, of a fish may also provide a glimpse into a lifestyle. For example, the yard-long, convoluted intestine of adult suckers aids in digestion of plant material and detritus. Detritus is decomposed material that collects on the surface and bottom of waterways. In contrast, predators such as bass and northern pikeminnow have a thin-walled, flexible stomach that expands to accommodate large prey like crayfish and juvenile salmon.

Scientists have determined that fishes can distinguish up to five visual properties of an object: size, shape, motion, color and contrast. Numerous studies have demonstrated the essential role of these visual cues for locating and capturing food. Sight is most important at close range because of the general murkiness of water and the way light is filtered. For example, red light is selectively removed after passing through the surface layer of water. Red is also the first color to fade at dusk and the last to appear at dawn. In comparison, blue light penetrates farthest in freshwater. It's a fact that fishermen predict fish interest by swapping lures and flies with different colors according to the time of the day and depth of presentation. We all have theories on how to catch fish.

Smell is also important to fishes. Ask anyone who fishes for catfishes and sturgeons how important the sense of smell is to their fishing success. Bait that does not signal its presence with a scent might as well not be used. In contrast, bait that release oils or "milk" will usually draw a hungry fish to the end of your line.

Some fish can "smell" chemical concentrations as low as 10 parts per billion or an amount equivalent to one drop in a kitchen sink full of water. The sense of smell does more than allow fish to find food. For example, fish use the sense of smell to detect and avoid pollutants. They also use smell to recognize and distinguish between members of the opposite sex. This ability comes in especially handy at spawning time.

Being able to detect odors present in the water column also has certain advantages when it comes to avoiding predators. Several species of minnow have special club cells in their skin that secrete an alarm substance if their skin is damaged. The release of this substance causes an immediate change in the schooling behavior of their peers. Salmon have been shown to be sensitive to the odor of bear paws and the human hand dipped in water.

It's not all about searching for food. Once fish find food, they must decide whether to eat it. This decision involves the sense of taste. Taste buds located in the mouth help fish manage their diet. Carp have a large pad on the roof of their mouth that serves to sort food items from non-edible debris. The common sucker has a series of small wart-like nubs, or papillae, on their fleshy lips that allow them to taste insects and algae while they graze on the bottom of rivers and lakes. Other fish have auxiliary taste buds on their whiskers or on their body surface. Bullheads not only use chin barbels to sniff out food, but their skin has receptor cells that can detect food.

Migration

Fishes migrate for several reasons. One reason might be to move in response to seasonal changes in temperature or flow. A fish might also migrate to avoid unfavorable environmental conditions or because of specific habitat requirements for spawning. Migration may be required to ensure successful reproduction and survival of young. Synchronized arrival of a population at a specific location can ensure reproductive success of that group. For example, migrating Pacific salmon move as a group toward their spawning grounds. Migration also allows fishes to colonize new areas. The more places a species exploits, the wider their distribution. In this manner, migration provides a survival advantage against unfavorable conditions that might occur in any one area.

There are several kinds of migration. Anadromous refers to fishes that spawn in freshwater, migrate to the ocean as juveniles, then return to their natal area as adults. An example of an anadromous species is Chinook salmon. Resident fish stay in freshwater their entire life cycle, but may migrate from one river system to another seasonally to feed, rear or spawn. Short-term migrations for feeding and spawning are common for resident fishes such as suckers and minnows. Generally, migration behavior has evolved to place adult fishes in a favorable place to spawn and juveniles in a favorable location to feed, grow and survive.

Several features of the environment may stimulate migration of fishes. The sun, moon and stars provide predictable reference points used by fishes to orient themselves relative to the surface of the earth. Several fishes, including sockeye salmon, use sun-compass orientation while homing or migrating. Effective use of the sun requires a fish have the sensory ability to detect the sun's position and a clock mechanism to compensate for the sun's apparent movement during the day.

The chemical landscape of the environment can also influence migration behavior of fishes. The types of minerals present in the water, salinity and dissolved oxygen concentration, and the presence of chemoreceptors, or chemical sensors, all play a part. The persistence of chemicals in water, in combination with water current, can carry information over long distances, far beyond the range of visual or mechanical stimuli.

Salmon and steelhead have an amazing ability related to the sense of smell called homing. Before juvenile salmon migrate to the Pacific Ocean, they become imprinted to the distinct chemistry of their home stream. Adult salmon use information obtained from this odor as a cue during the return migration. Their olfactory senses become finely tuned as they enter freshwater and approach the spawning season. An important consequence of successful homing is that it ensures salmon will return to spawn where conditions are most favorable to their survival.

Temperature changes also stimulate fish migration. Migratory fishes often respond to natural events causing temperature changes, including freshets and offshore winds. Because all fishes have a preferred range of temperatures, conditions that are too warm or too cool can limit their movement. Extreme temperatures may block entry into a river system. Daily and seasonal warming cycles also may separate species of fish according to depth.

Many fishes detect and respond to electric current using specialized sensory systems called electroreceptors. Directional information is provided from electrical currents such as those generated by objects moving through the earth's magnetic field. Magnetic information allows fishes to select a compass heading even when the sky is obscured. Examples of fishes known to change their activity patterns when subjected to changes in magnetic field are salmon and stickleback.

Available light has significant effects on both daily and seasonal activity patterns of fishes. The periodicity, direction and intensity of ambient light signal when to migrate, feed or spawn. Many predatory fishes, such as walleyes, are most active just before sunset and right at sunrise.

All fish have special mechanical receptors or nerve cells that respond to physical movement from water current, sound, body movement, pressure or gravity. These mechanical stimuli affect their behavior and include changes in barometric pressure that often precede or accompany weather changes, such as rainfall. A change in the weather will often trigger fish activity. Some of the most exciting trout fishing action I ever experienced occurred during a summer hailstorm.

Rheotaxis, or orientation to water currents, is largely a visual response in migratory fishes. This response orients a fish by allowing them to detect the direction of flow relative to fixed objects such as the stream bottom. Open pores that occur along the side of fishes, the lateral line, detect small-scale water movements and allows them to adjust their position. Imagine how stream fishes line up at the current interface to feed. Facing upstream into the current is known as positive rheotaxis. Downstream-migrating fish may respond to water current in a manner known as negative rheotaxis. Sound generated by natural phenomena such as rapids and waterfalls can provide landmark information to migrating fish. Hydrostatic pressure, as sensed by depth in the water column, may be used as a clue to orient and as the basis for vertical migration (Figure 4.6).

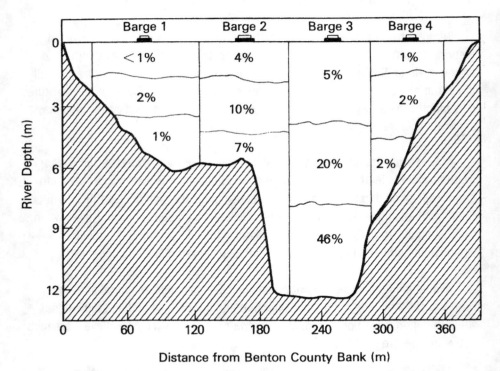

Figure 4.6. In the Hanford Reach of the Columbia River, juvenile Chinook salmon that migrated downstream during the spring occurred at higher proportion in the middle of the river and near the bottom. Most migration occurred at night, suggesting they responded to multiple environmental cues, including light, water depth and current (from Dauble et al 1989).

Species Interactions

Predation, competition and symbiosis are common behavioral interactions between fishes. Ultimately, these behaviors determine the composition of a fish community. They involve interactions with other fish species, members of the same population and other organisms.

Predation is one example of an important species interaction. An easy way to determine if predation has occurred is to examine the items in a fish's stomach. Most Columbia Basin predator fishes are non-native: walleye, bass and channel catfish. The most abundant native predator, northern pikeminnow, has developed a bad reputation. They are part of a bounty program designed to reduce predation on juvenile salmon. Most introduced predator species, on the other hand, are managed as sport fishes.

The outcome of a predator-prey interaction does not depend entirely on the choices of a predator. In most situations, prey behave in ways to protect themselves. Escape response differs widely between different species of fishes and can account for large differences in capture rate by predators. A common protective mechanism is taking cover in available structure. This behavior is not foolproof because large fish also use structure to employ a lie-and-wait strategy for taking prey. Other examples of predator avoidance include moving to shallow water, schooling and reducing their activity or "playing possum" in the presence of a predator. Characteristics of some fishes, such as spines, also may decrease their vulnerability to a predator. Not every fish is willing to choke down a three-spined stickleback.

Body coloration is another important aspect of fish survival. The challenge for fishes is to develop a color pattern that allows them to be seen by other members of their species during the breeding season and blend in with the background when they want to hide. Most fishes can modify their pigmentation to some extent, depending on the background. These changes may occur slowly or within seconds via the nervous system or hormonal control of special cells scattered throughout the skin. The main strategy behind this process is to make fish less conspicuous and therefore less vulnerable to attack from a predator.

Counter-shading is another common way for fishes to disguise themselves from predators. Being dark on the top helps them hide from an attack from above. This feature means fish-eating birds, such as great blue heron and the belted kingfisher, must rely on movement rather than color or contrast to make a decision to strike. Having light-colored bellies helps fish blend in better with the light sky when approached from below.

Charles Darwin defined competition as the demand of more than one organism for the same resource, such as food or space, in excess of supply. This concept establishes that two fish species are in competition only if common resource requirements are in limited supply. Don't mistake diet overlap as evidence that the same food item is in competition. Although both chiselmouth and suckers feed on periphyton in the Hanford Reach, there is plenty of this food source for all. Thus, the two species are not considered to be competitors. The same could be said for northern pikeminnow and rainbow trout feeding on abundant caddisfly. The end result of competition is a negative effect. That results in decreased growth or survival of the affected group of fishes or population.

Competition between two or more fish species is most intense when both or all occupy the same space and consume the same food concurrently. However, differences in behavior, daily activity patterns or habitat use may reduce competition. Two species may compete as juveniles and not as adults or vice versa. Because almost all fishes start out by feeding on plankton and other microorganisms, the potential for competition is greatest during early life stages.

Competitive interactions are not limited just to fishes. Fish-eating birds and piscivorous fishes compete when both rely on juvenile fish for a major part of their diet. Another example was mysids or opossum shrimps, a zooplankton predator, introduced to a freshwater lake in Idaho to enhance production of rainbow trout. This plan backfired because it depressed the growth of kokanee, landlocked sockeye salmon, which also were dependent on zooplankton.

Symbiosis, on the other hand, is a term that refers to an association of two fish populations that provide an advantage to one or both species. Symbiosis may be simply defined as "living together." A common symbiotic interaction between fishes in freshwater environments is multispecies schooling. An example of symbiosis occurs when juvenile suckers and minnows form large schools in the shallows of Mid-Columbia reservoirs in summer. This behavior provides an advantage for individual fish confronted by a predator. As these same species grow, they segregate and/or become territorial. The latter behavior makes them more vulnerable to predators because individuals are easier to "pick off."

These behaviors are but a few examples of how fish respond to living parts of their environment. In the next chapter, I discuss how fish respond to environmental conditions such as temperature, dissolved oxygen and flow. Collectively, it's a combination of both living (biotic) and nonliving (abiotic) factors that shape the structure of aquatic ecosystems and the makeup of local fish communities.

•••

Each individual has a range of environmental conditions within which it can be successful."

—Charles Warren, *Biology and Water Pollution Control*, 1971

The Columbia River carves a deep gorge through the Cascade Range, at Crown Point State Park, Oregon.

"The river as plaintiff speaks for the ecological unit of life that is part of it."

—William O. Douglas, *Sierra Club v. Morton*, 1972

Chapter 5. Environmental Factors Affecting Fish Distribution and Abundance

In any environment, one or more controlling factors influence where fishes live and grow. Two of the most important limiting factors are temperature and dissolved oxygen. These characteristics are important because they affect basic metabolism, reproduction and growth. Water flow volume or discharge is also important for stream fishes because it affects habitat features such as water velocity and depth. Substrate provides cover, is important for spawning and provides a surface for food organisms to colonize. Water quality, including concentration of salts, nutrients and pollutants, also affects fish distribution and abundance.

A guiding principle is that all fishes exist within a range of physical and chemical conditions. These conditions comprise their habitat requirements. Habitat requirements are what a fish needs to successfully live, grow and reproduce. When conditions change, fishes must adapt, move to a more favorable environment or face reduced success in growth and survival. Habitat requirements are dependent on a species' life stage and season of the year. Although a certain habitat feature may be important for a species' survival, a suite of environmental conditions covering an entire life cycle must be met for fishes to thrive in a particular location. Having a range of habitat types available increases the probability that a species will find suitable conditions to grow and reproduce.

Water Temperature

All fishes are cold blooded. Scientists call cold-blooded animals "poikilotherms" (from the Greek *poikilos*, meaning changeable) because their body temperature fluctuates with their surroundings. Thus, at any given time and place, a fish's body temperature is very close to the temperature of the water.

Water has a unique property of being densest at around 39 degrees Fahrenheit. This property makes ice float and creates an unusual temperature gradient in lakes and ponds. Hence, lakes and streams freeze from the top down. This means water is always a few degrees warmer at the bottom of iced-over lakes. It's a different situation for rivers and streams. Flowing water is more uniformly mixed due to turbulent flow. Large streams rarely get so cold as to completely freeze over (Figure 5.1). Indeed, the last time the lower Columbia River froze from bank to bank was in 1930.

Figure 5.1. Columbia River frozen over (Special Collections & University Archives, University of Oregon Libraries, ORU_PH035_6035)

Because fish cannot adjust their body temperature, every species has an optimum temperature range where life cycle activities are most efficient. Beyond this range are unfavorably low or high temperatures. So, fishes have strategies that allow them to cope. As water temperatures drop in the fall, they may form aggregations or groups. This behavior offers survival benefits from predators when low temperatures inhibit swimming. Another strategy when temperatures are low is to hide in the streambed or other cover. Juvenile smallmouth bass often hide deep in cracks of large boulders during the winter "hibernation" period. Other fishes move into deeper areas of ponds, lakes or reservoirs where water is warmer.

Warm water also can be a challenge. Fishes may be prevented from colonizing warm waters because temperatures are too high or because warm water impedes reproduction. Salmon are especially sensitive to high water temperature. For example, fall Chinook salmon delay their migration into the Yakima and Okanogan rivers in late summer when water temperatures exceed 75 F. Upstream migrating steelhead "dip in," or take up, temporary residence in cool tributaries of the lower Columbia River in the summer, such as the Wind and White Salmon rivers. Area fishermen capitalize on this behavior by frequenting lower stretches of these streams.

A common situation for lakes in the summer is having a warm surface layer separated from a deeper, cold layer. The region in which the temperature changes markedly over a short distance is called a thermocline (Figure 5.2). Thermal gradients in lakes are predictable. Kokanee use them as orienting stimuli. In contrast, rivers and streams do not normally vertically stratify because of turbulent mixing, although there may be lateral differences in temperature, as the sun warms shallow shoreline areas, for example. Daily temperatures at the upper part of a stream may be fairly uniform, but downstream temperatures may fluctuate widely, particularly in summer.

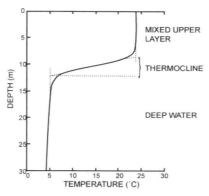

Figure 5.2. Thermocline (author figure)

All rivers and lakes have seasonal variations in temperature as well as horizontal and vertical temperature gradients. Seasonal cycles of water warming and cooling trigger spawning and migration. All fish depend on the season to produce young at a favorable time. Thus, the geographic range of a fish species coincides with areas where specific climatic events occur.

The development cycle of aquatic insects that fish feed on also responds to water temperature. For example, caddisfly transform from their larval stage and emerge as adults at the same time that juvenile fall Chinook salmon begin to move offshore and feed on the surface. The primary controlling factor in this classic example of nature's synchrony is water temperature.

Dissolved Oxygen

Oxygen is needed by all aquatic organisms to "breathe." Concentration of oxygen in natural waters and its availability to fish varies widely according to temperature. The amount of oxygen held in equilibrium decreases as water temperature increases. Smaller bodies of water are subject to greater fluctuation of dissolved oxygen than large water bodies.

In the Potholes Reservoir of eastern Washington and other inland lakes and reservoirs with abundant aquatic vegetation, photosynthesis may lead to super-saturated oxygen conditions by day. But at night, respiration by plants may reduce dissolved oxygen levels. Decomposition of algae and large plants also uses up oxygen. In the summer, thermal stratification of deep lakes results in water layers with different oxygen concentrations. These conditions can affect fish distribution.

An increase in water temperature increases fish metabolism and oxygen uptake. Fish compensate for low oxygen concentrations by pumping blood faster and increasing their breathing rate. Consequently, they expend more energy to maintain the same level of activity.

Certain species of fish, like salmon and trout, are less tolerant of low levels of dissolved oxygen than others, such as carp. Differences in tolerance related to life stage also exist. Fish eggs are relatively resistant to low dissolved oxygen concentrations, but after hatching, their sensitivity generally increases.

Discharge

Stream discharge or flow per unit time, is dictated by the amount of rainfall and snowmelt that a watershed receives. Discharge is monitored throughout the Columbia Basin using stream gauges located at standard locations. The discharge pattern of the Columbia and Snake rivers is complicated because storage reservoirs high in the system retain and release water according to power and irrigation demands. In contrast, unregulated streams respond to climatic events in a more predictable manner. The seasonal discharge pattern for a river or stream is called its hydrograph (Figure 5.3).

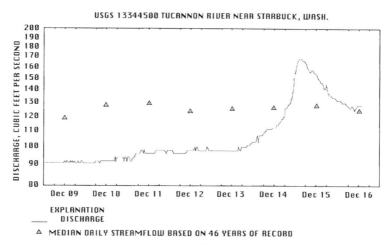

Figure 5.3. Tucannon River hydrograph (adapted from http://waterdata.usgs.gov, March 2007)

The longitudinal gradient, or gradient of a stream, is a measure of how much it drops in elevation from the headwaters to a downstream point. Stream gradient is largely responsible for changes in water velocity such as those occurring in the rapids of a large river. Water velocities also change vertically and laterally in streams and rivers. For example, highest velocities occur near the surface and at mid-channel. Fish often seek low velocity areas near the shoreline and at the bottom of streams to conserve energy.

Water current influences the energy requirements of fishes during migration. Migrating salmon and steelhead expend more energy swimming through areas of high velocity than when resting. In contrast, juvenile salmon move downstream with less energy where high velocities are present. They take advantage of this condition by migrating during spring freshets. Resident stream fishes reside where they can best conserve energy with an eye toward feeding opportunity and predator avoidance.

Columbia and Snake river dams have created an interesting trade-off for migrating salmon and steelhead related to velocity. It takes several days longer for smolts to migrate to the Pacific Ocean than before dams were built because river reaches were changed to slow-moving reservoirs. Interestingly, adult salmon and steelhead now migrate through reservoirs faster than through riverine reaches. Adult Chinook salmon returning to spawning areas in the Snake River average 35 miles per day through slack water behind dams compared to 10 to 20 miles per day when swimming through flowing sections.

In general, a stream supports more species and greater numbers of fish as it flows from its headwaters to downstream locations. As a watershed collects discharge from the surrounding landscape, a stream deepens and spreads out over a larger area. This increased discharge allows fish to migrate more freely and helps limit fluctuations in water temperature.

River flows can be dynamic. With high water, silt and sand are scoured from the stream bank and washed downstream. High velocities and associated turbidity from floods scour the surface of rocks, removing algae and insects that live there. Flooding may also disperse fish and other aquatic creatures downstream into different, unfavorable habitat. If changes in river stage are rapid, fish can get stranded along the riverbank as water recedes.

All streams benefit from flooding though. Channel features such as river bars and riffle-pool sequences are formed and maintained by high discharge. Floods also aid in the process of nutrient flow. Decomposing vegetation that accumulates on riverbanks during dry periods rapidly enter into solution when flooding begins. This process is important for maintaining stream ecosystems. Scientists call such events a "flood-pulse."

Side channels and tributaries provide safe havens for fish during periods of rising water because they drop and clear sooner. Knowing this behavior, I angle for trout in feeder creeks when large streams are high and roily. Rising water also induces movement of migratory fishes. Fishermen capitalize on knowledge that adult steelhead migrate into tributaries of the Columbia and Snake rivers following the first high water event in the fall.

The flip side of a flood is drought and resulting low flow. Low stream discharge can be a serious challenge for fishes that live in small tributary streams, particularly where water is withdrawn for seasonal irrigation use. In some situations, fish respond to low flows by seeking refuge in deep pools or by migrating downstream. These strategies have their limits, however. Their displacement can lead to competition for food and space, poor water quality or increased exposure to predators.

> **How is the flow or discharge of a stream determined?**
>
> It's actually fairly simple. For this exercise we use English measurements. You first need to determine the cross-sectional area of the stream, i.e., stream width (W) times the average depth (Z). Stream width is the bank-to-bank distance. To determine average depth, measure several locations along the channel cross section. A crude but effective measurement of velocity (V) can be made by timing how fast an orange drifts through a known distance of stream. This exercise provides an estimate of the water's velocity expressed as feet per second (ft/sec). The total stream width (ft) multiplied by the average stream depth (ft) times the velocity (ft/sec) provides an estimate of stream discharge (Q). The formula is summarized as W x Z x V = Q, yielding a value in cubic feet per second (cfs) or ft^3/sec.

Substrate

Substrate is the material that makes up the bottom of rivers and lakes. The nature of a water body's substrate is determined primarily by the minerals of the watershed whether deposited during past glacial events or from upstream tributaries, and the pattern of water movement. Substrate is usually classified according to grain size or diameter. Fine-grained material includes silt, sand and clay, while coarser-grained material might be cobble (i.e., fist-sized rock) or boulders. Bedrock is also commonly found in Columbia Basin waterways. Each type of substrate has a purpose.

Substrate affects the spawning success of fish such as salmon and trout that make nests (redds) in gravel- and cobble-sized rocks. For egg incubation to be successful, intra-gravel flow is needed. Too much silt or fine-grained sediment can clog interstitial spaces and smother developing eggs and embryos.

Substrate provides a surface for algae to colonize, in addition to being essential habitat for aquatic insects and other small invertebrates on which fish feed. The availability of substrate of different sizes and shapes provides a wider diversity of aquatic plants and animals, including fishes, to be present.

Salinity

Because fish gills are in constant contact with water they must maintain a balance between essential salts in their blood and those found in the environment. The blood of all freshwater fishes is more concentrated than the water they live in. This means they tend to gain water across the gills. To compensate, freshwater fishes pass large amounts of dilute urine, up to 10 times more than their saltwater counterparts (Figure 5.4).

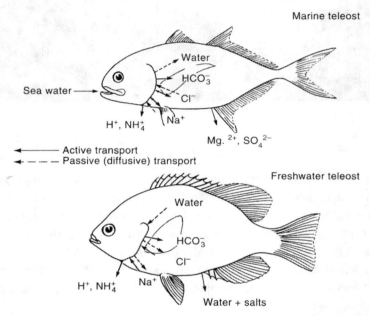

Figure 5.4 Schematic of how active and passive saltwater transport mechanisms differ between freshwater and saltwater fishes (modified from Wooten 1990)

Anadromous fishes such as salmon provide an excellent example of saltwater regulation. The transformation process from fry to smolt helps salmon prepare for a dramatic change regulated by their pituitary gland. Environmental triggers for this change include increasing day length and rising water temperature.

When smolts migrate from natal streams to the Pacific Ocean, they enter an entirely new environment, one with much higher salt concentrations. So how do smolts switch gears and adapt to life in salt water? Largely, it has to do with special salt-secreting cells that form in their gills. The estuary, or mixing zone where the river meets the sea, provides time for smolts to adjust. The reverse is true for adult salmon returning to freshwater to spawn. All migratory fish species spend extra time in the estuary adapting to changes in salinity. This process is similar to how mountain climbers stage activities in order to tolerate low oxygen levels at high altitude. The process of fishes adapting to a change in their environment is known as acclimation.

Columbia Basin fishes with the ability to move from freshwater to salt water include salmon, steelhead, eulachon, white and green sturgeon, Pacific lamprey, and American shad. Fishes that migrate from rivers to the ocean as part of their normal life cycle are versatile enough to reach equilibrium with their new environment in as little as one to two days. Other fishes are restricted from entering salt water because they can only regulate saltwater balance within narrow limits and vice versa. This is why you will never see a sucker in the Pacific Ocean or a flounder in the Yakima River.

Water Quality

Examples of water quality issues in the Columbia Basin include storm water return from urban environments, industrial discharges and agricultural runoff. Pollutants from these activities, alone or in combination, affect fish survival. This section provides a brief summary of a very complicated topic.

Fishes have a tolerance range for each type of environmental pollutant. If the concentration of a pollutant exceeds their physiological limit, they will be stressed or die. The additive effects of pollutants with another environmental stress, such as elevated temperature or reduced dissolved oxygen, also can be a factor in fish survival. Excess nutrient loading, in conjunction with high temperature, led to oxygen depletion and a massive fish kill in the lower Yakima River. Agricultural and industrial practices impaired water quality in the Willamette River, although conditions improved markedly after the 1950s.

Pollutants of concern in the Columbia Basin include heavy metals from past mining activity, pesticides and herbicides from agricultural sources, polychlorobiphenyl compounds (PCBs), and industrial products such as those found in pulp mill effluent. For the most part, contaminants from these activities are local, but many are transported downstream and deposited in stream sediments. The Columbia River is less vulnerable to impacts from pollutants than smaller water bodies because of its large dilution factor. Similarly, impacts of pollutants to streams and rivers are more transient than impacts to ponds and lakes because of turnover.

The risk of a specific pollutant to fishes is both a function of its concentration and duration of exposure. Where contaminants are found in the environment affect whether fish are exposed via their diet, sediments or in the water column (Figure 5.5). Some fishes may detect and avoid harmful conditions in a manner that ultimately affects their distribution and survival. This response may be beneficial if they seek out and successfully adapt to new habitats. Conversely, avoidance can be detrimental if it excludes them from habitat needed for growth and reproduction.

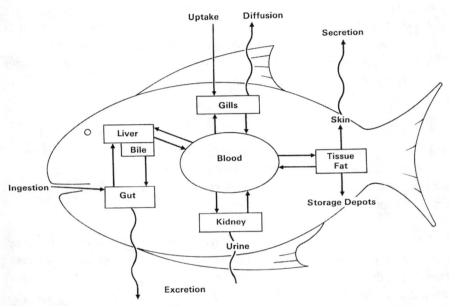

Figure 5.5. Conceptual diagram of how fish take up pollutants via food, water or sediments and processes by which contaminants are stored and excreted from the body (author figure).

The most significant changes to rivers and streams of the Columbia Basin in the past century include alteration of streamflow, velocity and temperature. The capacity of many tributary streams to support native fish populations has been reduced further because of water withdrawal, industrial activities and domestic water use practices. The overall response of fish populations to changes in water quality has been reduced populations of sensitive species and changes in the mix of species.

Looking ahead, what can be expected from climate change? How will this phenomenon affect fishes? Fish will experience the effect of global warming in different ways. One relates to the timing of snowmelt. Snowpack drives the hydrological cycle in the Columbia Basin. Increased air temperature will melt snow sooner and faster.

Reservoir operations might slow the rate of runoff in the Columbia and Snake rivers, but only within limits of storage capacity. Small streams will dry up as air temperature increases, leading to loss of fish production. Another impact will be increased water temperatures. We can expect an increase in both population and diversity of "exotic" or introduced species tolerant of warm water, such as bass, catfish and carp, and decreased numbers of native cold-water species such as trout, salmon and sculpins.

Is that fish safe to eat?

In 1991, the U.S. Environmental Protection Agency (EPA) entered into an agreement with the Columbia River Inter-Tribal Fish Commission and its four member tribes to analyze fish tissues for contaminants in order to better understand the likelihood of tribal exposures through fish consumption. Five species of anadromous fish and six species of resident fish were collected from 24 sites from 1996 to 2002. The most frequently detected contaminants included metals, DDE and PCBs.

Salmon, steelhead and rainbow trout had the lowest levels of contaminants, while bottom-feeding species like white sturgeon, largescale sucker, and mountain whitefish had higher levels. Concentrations in the meat were generally about one-fifth of those found in whole body (includes guts, skeleton and skin) samples. Chemical concentrations were generally lower than levels reported from the 1970s.

In certain instances, fish consumption advisories have been placed. These advisories, suggesting that consumption of target species be limited to one to two meals per month, were designed to lower exposure risk to vulnerable groups (i.e., pregnant women and young children). Examples of recent advisories include fish from Lake Roosevelt, the lower Snake and the Willamette rivers for mercury and the lower Walla Walla River for PCBs. Carp, walleyes and smallmouth bass are among species of concern for these locations.

Health risk associated with eating a potentially contaminated fish depends on several factors including the concentration of a contaminant in edible tissue, the type of fish eaten, the amount and frequency of fish in one's diet, and the body weight of the person eating the fish. Post-harvest procedures such as trimming skin and fat from muscle fillets and cooking will decrease risk of exposure.

"The body form of a fish can be used in quick appraisal of its way of life."

—Carl E. Bond, *Biology of Fishes*, 1996

"We give fish names as a way organizing our knowledge about them."

–P.B. Moyle, *Fish*, 1993

Chapter 6. How to Identify Fishes

To be able to tell one fish species from another, you must first answer the question, "What is a fish?" Not all animals with fins that swim in the water are fish. Lewis and Clark struggled with that concept more than 200 years ago when they traveled to the Pacific Coast as evidenced by the journal entry of March 13, 1806: "The Porpus (sic) is common on this coast and as far up the river as the water is brackish. The Indians Sometimes gig them and always eat the flesh of this fish when they Can precure (sic) it." There is no reason to confuse a marine mammal with a fish if you know what features to look for.

Generally stated, a fish is a cold-blooded vertebrate, an animal with a backbone that cannot regulate its body temperature. It lives in water, has fins and breathes with gills. This definition distinguishes fishes from warm-blooded aquatic mammals such as whales, porpoises and seals, and also from cold-blooded aquatic animals like reptiles and amphibians. Another important fact is that not all fishes have scales. For example, catfishes are smooth-bodied. If you are confused because salamanders also have gills, recall that they have no fins.

At the highest level of classification, fish species are grouped as those with jaws and those without. Another distinction is between "cartilaginous" fishes and those with a bony skeleton. Both former groups are considered ancient forms and the latter are more modern. An example of a jawless cartilaginous fish from the Columbia Basin are lampreys. The white sturgeon is also cartilaginous, but they have jaws. All other fishes from the region have jaws and bony skeletons. More information on the evolution and classification of fish can be found in references listed in the back of this book.

Once you have a general idea of what different groups of fishes look like, the next step is to figure out the difference between closely related species. So what is a species? Fish species are formally classified by Latin names that are recognized internationally. The Linnaean system of classification, developed by the father of modern taxonomy, Carl Linnaeus, dates back to 1758. This system uses both genus and species names. The generic name or genus of fishes, and all other animal groups, is always capitalized, but the species name is not. Both names are usually italicized. *Oncorhynchus tshawytscha* is the Latin name for Chinook salmon. Brown trout is *Salmo trutta*. Memorize a few of the more interesting scientific names and impress your friends. Latin does not have to be a dead language.

This book uses family as the first level of classification. A key to genus and species follows the family key in chapter 7. The biology of all common fishes of the Mid-Columbia, in addition to more detail on characteristics of closely related species, is described in chapter 8.

Care and Handling of Fishes

Most species of fish can be collected, identified and released alive with proper care and handling. When possible, keep a fish in the water when unhooking or examining it. If a fish is deeply hooked or bleeding, and you intend to release it, cut the leader. Don't squeeze the body or hold a fish by the gills. It is best to keep all fishes in the water while they are being released. Take a picture of interesting specimens as a reminder of important characteristics that will otherwise be forgotten. Include an object in the photo that provides a frame of reference for body dimensions.

Fish that are preserved by freezing or by storing in an alcohol solution will eventually lose their color. However, preservation allows for additional study that can provide their correct classification with more confidence.

Observing Fishes

There are many ways to observe fishes in their natural habitat. Snorkeling in small streams or in the shallows of rivers and lakes is one way. Try turning over rocks to find sculpins and other sedentary species. Small minnows such as dace and shiners are often attracted to fine materials that are displaced. Wading along the shoreline is another method used to locate fishes, although water clarity and depth may make accurate identification difficult.

A useful tool for observing fishes in natural habitats is an underwater camera. A good one can be purchased for around $200 from Cabela's or a local sporting goods store. Migrating salmon and steelhead, in addition to a variety of resident fish species, can be viewed in fish ladders or visitor centers at large dams on the Columbia and Snake rivers.

General Features of Fishes

To correctly identify a fish, it is necessary to know its different body parts. A good approach is to think about how birds are identified. All experienced birdwatchers learn to look for key features that distinguish a "little brown job," as my oldest brother calls them, from what might be identified as a house finch or white-crowned sparrow, for example. Similarly, fisheries biologists look for differences in snout length, where fins are placed or body shape.

Fishes from the Columbia Basin come in a variety of shapes that relate to their swimming habits. Many fish, like trout and suckers, are cylindrical in cross-section, being thicker in the front half and tapering to the tail. This shape is considered to be "streamlined." Other groups of fish, such as bass, sunfishes and shad, are more flattened from side to side. Catfishes tend to be flattened downward in the head region.

Mid-Columbia fish species also come in a wide range of colors and spotting patterns. Coloration allows fish to blend in with the background and individuals to recognize their relatives. As a fish matures, its color often changes. Males and females are also often markedly different in coloration during the spawning season. Because many fish change colors during their life cycle or as a result of their background, the use of color or spotting patterns to sort closely related species is not encouraged.

The following section of this chapter describes and compares various features of fishes. Figures 6.1 and 6.2 are provided as a general guide to locating and identifying external features of trout and largemouth bass, respectively.

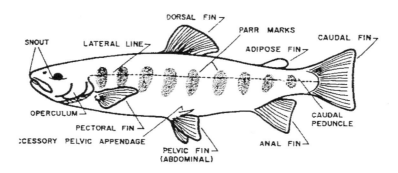

Figure 6.1. General body features of a rainbow trout (from C.E. Bond, *Keys to Oregon Fishes*, Corvallis, Oregon, 1994)

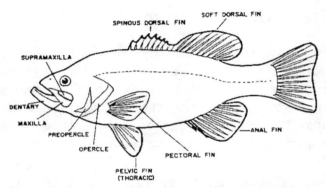

Figure 6.2. General body features of a largemouth bass (from C.E. Bond, *Keys to Oregon Fishes*, Corvallis, Oregon, 1994)

External Anatomy

Several features of external anatomy are important for distinguishing one fish from another. This section describes the most important of these features.

Fins

Fins are accessory organs of locomotion. Structurally, fins are outgrowths of skin supported by soft or spiny rays. Most fish have two sets of paired fins and three unpaired, or single, fins. The location, number and type of fins are often related to a fish's body shape.

Pectoral fins are normally located high on fish bodies. They range in shape from long and pointed to broad and rounded. Pelvic fins act as stabilizers to assist pectoral fins in turning and braking. Pelvic fin placement may be low relative to the pectoral fins or more ventral in more modern groups like sunfishes (see Figure 6.3). Both dorsal and anal (ventral) fins provide stability, somewhat like a ship rudder, while swimming.

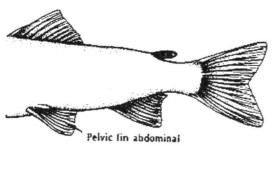

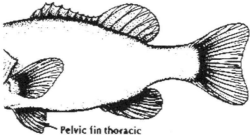

Figure 6.3. Location of pelvic fins relative to dorsal fin (from C.J.D. Brown, *Fishes of Montana*, Bozeman, Montana, 1971)

The primary function of the caudal, or tail fin, is to provide thrust (Figure 6.4). Its shape is often a distinguishing characteristic. For example, white sturgeons have a heterocercal tail, or one where the upper lobe is much longer than the lower lobe. Other fishes have a forked tail or rounded caudal fin. The adipose fin is a small, fleshy appendage located between the dorsal fin and tail and only found on salmon, trout, whitefish, sand roller and catfish.

Some fins possess both spiny and soft rays (Figure 6.5). This feature is commonly used to distinguish among closely related species of bass and sunfish (family Centrarchidae). This group of fishes is commonly referred to as "spiny-rays" because they have spines in the leading edge of their dorsal and anal fins.

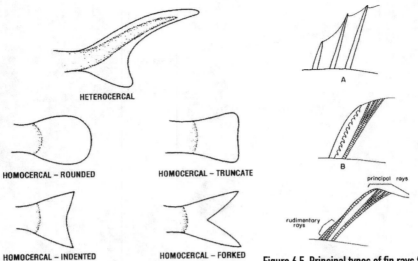

Figure 6.4. Tail shapes for fishes (from R.S. Wydoski and R.R. Whitney, *Inland Fishes of Washington*, Seattle, 2003)

Figure 6.5. Principal types of fin rays for fishes (from R.S. Wydoski and R.R. Whitney, *Inland Fishes of Washington*, Seattle, 2003)

Mouth and teeth

A fish's mouth shape, size, position and teeth are all related to feeding habits. Most fishes have mouths that are either turned down, ventral or inferior, or terminal, pointing in a forward position (Figure 6.6). Other variations in mouth position may include subterminal or superior.

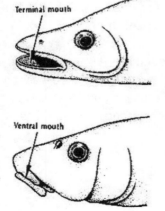

Figure 6.6. Mouth positions of a northern pikeminnow and a sucker (from C.J.D. Brown, *Fishes of Montana*, Bozeman, Montana, 1971)

The types and location of teeth often help distinguish one species of fish from another. Teeth present on both the upper and lower jaws and on the tongue usually function to hold prey. Certain species, like minnows and suckers, have teeth in their throat, pharyngeal teeth, which are used to break up and grind food (Figure 6.7).

The jaw teeth of adult salmon elongate, and males develop large heads and jaws during the spawning season. The upper jaw of salmon greatly enlarges and extends downward, forming a distinct snout. In contrast, breeding trout and chars develop a hook, or "kype," at the tip of their lower jaw. Francis Day introduced this term in 1887, perhaps through a misspelling of the word kip – meaning an upward turn of the nose. These changes provide male salmon and trout with formidable weapons when they battle for a mate.

Scales

Most species of fish have a series of thin, bony or fibrous plates known as scales embedded in their skin. As fish grow, their scales increase in size by adding fresh material to the outer margin in concentric rings known as circuli. The distance between circuli is dependent on growth rates. The patterns of growth can be used to age the fish, much like counting rings on a tree.

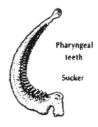

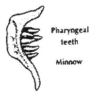

Figure 6.7. Pharyngeal teeth of minnows and suckers (from C.J.D. Brown, *Fishes of Montana*, Bozeman, Montana, 1971)

There is a wide diversity in the number and type of fish scales. Scales may range from armor-like, bony plates to a dense covering of thin, flexible scales, to no scales at all. Fish species have four main types of scales covering their body: cycloid, ctenoid, ganoid and placoid. Cycloid scales are circular in shape and found on salmon, trout, suckers and minnows. Ctenoid scales are shaped like a garden spade having a serrated edge. Spiny-rayed fishes like bass, bluegill and walleye have ctenoid scales. Figure 6.8 shows how circuli appear for these two scale types.

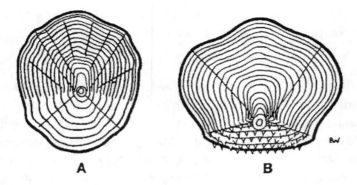

Figure 6.8. Cycloid and ctenoid scale (from C.E. Bond, *Keys to Oregon Fishes*, Corvallis, Oregon, 1994)

The other two types of fish scales are less common. Ganoid scales are rhomboid shaped. Both sturgeons and sticklebacks have modified versions of ganoid scales called scutes. These bony plates line the sides of their body like medieval armor. Sharks and rays are the only fishes with placoid scales. Placoid scales are similar to teeth in their structure. They lend a raspy texture to shark skin and are sometimes referred to as dermal denticles.

All fish scales "umbricate," or overlap along the body similar to shingles on a roof. This arrangement protects fishes from collision with underwater objects and also results in a favorable hydrodynamic situation when they swim. Some fish have evolved without scales, for example channel catfish. As a result, their skin is thicker than those of fish covered with scales.

Special scales located along the side of fish have tiny holes or canals in them that allow water to flow through to a sensory system. These scales form a pattern known as the lateral line. One theory is that this lateral-line system responds to stimuli such as water movement and sound waves. Some fish have a lateral line that extends from the back edge of the gill cover in a straight line to the insertion of caudal fin rays. Other fish may have an irregular or broken pattern of lateral line pores.

Internal Anatomy

This section describes the general features of the internal anatomy of fish or what is often referred to as their "guts." Knowing the various organs of fish is useful for distinguishing some species from another in addition to understanding how they respond to the environment.

Gill structure

A gill consists of a crescent-shaped, arched bone that supports a series of tiny, comb-like bones on the inside or leading edge (gill rakers) and red flexible tissue (gill filaments) on the outside of the arch. The number and length of gill rakers is related to the fish's feeding habits. Respiration, or oxygen exchange, occurs when water moves past gill filaments highly saturated with blood vessels. Oxygen exchange is highly efficient in fishes because blood flows across the gill filaments in a direction opposite that of water. This process is known as "counter-current" exchange.

Digestive system

The internal organs of digestion consist of a stomach, intestine and associated structures. These organs may either be distinct in shape as in trout or more uniform with no obvious difference along the length of the digestive tract as in minnows and suckers. Herbivores, or plant-eating fish, such as suckers, tend to have a longer digestive tract than piscivores, or fish-eating fish. The liver is another organ of importance. It functions in digestion and detoxification of pollutants. The kidney is a blackish strip of tissue that lays along the fish's backbone and assists in maintaining water balance.

Swim bladder

The swim bladder, a balloon-like organ used in most fishes to regulate buoyancy, is located between the intestinal tract and the kidney. Swim bladders are of two basic types. Physostomous bladders are connected to the gut by a pneumatic duct. This duct is open to the outside and allows salmon and trout to rapidly inflate their swim bladder by gulping air at the water's surface or deflate it by "burping." In contrast, fish with a closed, or physoclistous, swim bladder, like bass and sunfishes, have a special circulatory system for regulating the amount of air in their swim bladder. Sculpins are one of few area fishes with no swim bladder. As a result, sculpins cannot maintain themselves in the water column without swimming vigorously. This limitation is the main reason that sculpins reside at the bottom of area waterways.

Reproductive organs

The organs of reproduction are called ovaries in the female and testes in the male. These organs lay alongside the kidneys and are connected externally by a pair of tubes that open near the anus. Ovaries produce eggs and testes produce sperm. The relative size and color of the ovaries and testes is an indication of the level of maturity. Mature eggs may range from yellow to red-orange in color. Testes usually turn from reddish to creamy white as they grow in size and mature.

How to Count and Measure Characteristics of Fishes

This section provides specific detail on taxonomic methods known as measurement (morphometry) and counting (meristics). Because a fish's body shape may change as it grows, meristic data are considered more conclusive than morphometric data when attempting to distinguish between two or more closely related species. Meristic features rarely change as fishes grow or mature, but the morphometry or relative shape of the body may change over time.

Figure 6.9 indicates principal points of measurement and counting for a largemouth bass. These locations are similar for most other fish species.

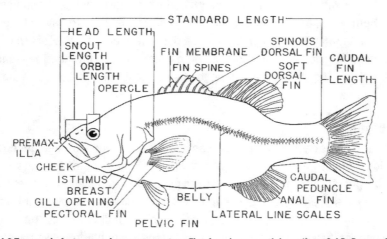

Figure 6.9 Taxonomic features and measurement profiles for a largemouth bass (from C.J.D. Brown, *Fishes of Montana*, Bozeman, Montana, 1971)

The body of a fish is separated into three main parts: head, trunk and tail. The head includes the portion from the tip of the snout to the back edge of the opercle, or gill cover. The trunk is from this point to the anal opening, and the tail is from the anal opening to the back edge of the caudal fin. Measuring between these distances is often helpful in identifying a species. For example, a species may be identified by the relationship between head length and body length. Fish species having large heads relative to body length have a larger value when the ratio is expressed as a percentage of the total.

Three primary measurements relate to the body length of a fish: total, standard and fork. Total length is what fishermen measure to get credit for maximum size. This measurement is the straight-line distance from the tip of the snout to the back of the tail fin. Standard length is the distance from the snout to the tip of the hypural plate at the base of the caudal fin. Taxonomists typically use standard length because the condition of the caudal fin can be variable, particularly in museum specimens. The hypural plate marks the end of the vertebral column and can be located by bending the caudal fin and looking for a crease near the base of the tail. Length of the caudal peduncle is the straight-line distance from the end of the hypural plate to the insertion or back edge of the anal fin. Fork length is the distance from the snout to the fork of the caudal fin.

There are two important depth measurements for distinguishing between fish species. Body depth is the greatest depth of the body, not including fins. This is the straight-line distance perpendicular to the leading edge of the dorsal fin. The measurement extends from the top of the fish to the midline of its belly. Depth of the caudal peduncle is the minimum depth of the region between the end of the hypural plate and insertion of the anal fin.

Fish are also identified by the type and number of fin rays. There are three main types of fin rays: spiny, spinous and soft. Spiny rays, sometimes referred to as spines, are usually stiff and sharp. They are unsegmented and never branched. Spinous rays may be stiff and with sharp barbs on the posterior edge. Spinous rays are present only in carps, goldfishes and catfishes. Soft rays are usually branched and segmented, but often visible only if observed under magnification.

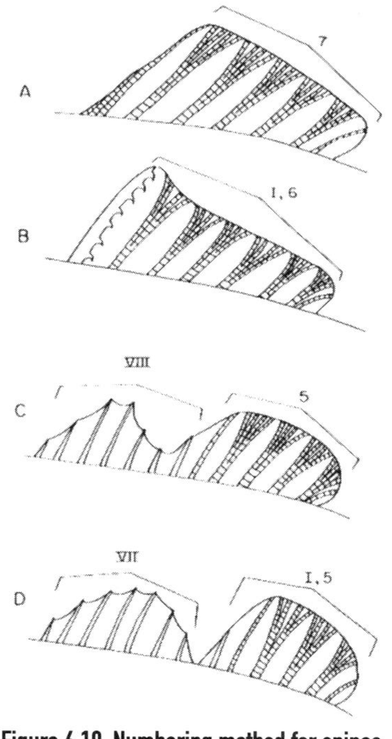

Figure 6.10. Numbering method for spines and soft rays of fishes (from R.S. Wydoski and R.R. Whitney, *Inland Fishes of Washington*, Seattle, 2003)

When counting the spiny rays of a fin, all spines are counted regardless of size. The spine count is usually shown in Roman numerals. In contrast, soft ray counts are recorded in Arabic numerals (refer to Figure 6.10). In counting the soft rays of a dorsal or anal fin, include only principal rays. The short, unbranched rays along the leading edge of the fin are considered rudimentary (see Figure 6.5) and are usually excluded. All soft rays of paired fins are counted, including rudimentary rays.

Counting fish scales is another species identification method. The number of scales in a row, the number of rows and their relative position combine to form a scale pattern characteristic for a species. Two main types of scale counts are commonly used to distinguish among fishes. Scales on the lateral line is the number of scales lying on the lateral line from the shoulder girdle, cleithrum, to the end of the hypural plate or origin of the caudal fin (refer to Figure 6.9). The most anterior scale in the count, or the first one counted, is where the body ends – often under the opercle or gill cover. The number of scales above the lateral line is the oblique row that starts with the first scale in front of the origin of the dorsal fin and continues down to, but not including, the lateral line.

Connected to the upper end of the intestine near the stomach of some fish is a series of finger-like appendages called pyloric caeca (refer to Figure 6.11). Pyloric caeca are thought to function in digestion with numbers present varying widely from species to species. Their number is often used to distinguish between various salmon and trout.

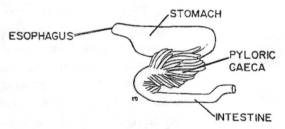

Figure 6.11. Pyloric caeca of a rainbow trout (from C.E. Bond, *Keys to Oregon Fishes*, Corvallis, Oregon, 1994)

Both the number and length of gill rakers may be used to distinguish between closely related species of fishes (refer to Figure 6.12). Lake whitefish and kokanee, fishes that filter-feed in the water column, have extra-long gill rakers that appear as comb-like bones on their gill arches. In contrast, the northern pikeminnow, a predator fish, has short, stubby gill rakers.

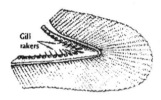

Figure 6.12. Gill arch (from C.J.D. Brown, *Fishes of Montana*, Bozeman, Montana, 1971)

A final characteristic used to distinguish between families of fishes relates to whether branchiostegal membranes are attached to the isthmus – that narrow bridge of flesh connecting the lower jaw region to the trunk of the body. These membranes connect the series of long, slender bones near the ventral or lower margin of the gill cover, or opercle. The branchiostegal membranes are either attached directly to the isthmus or extend forward without attachment to the isthmus (Figure 6.13). American shad are an example of a fish having branchiostegals free from the isthmus. In contrast, suckers and minnows have attached branchiostegal membranes.

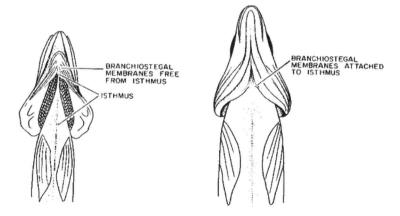

Figure 6.13. Branchiostegal membranes (from R.S. Wydoski and R.R. Whitney, *Inland Fishes of Washington*, Seattle, 2003)

"We have endeavored to avoid, on one hand, unnatural associations, and on the other, subdivision beyond reasonable limits."
—D.S. Jordan and C.H. Gilbert,
Synopsis of the Fishes of North America, 1882

"While many of the fishes in a given section are easily recognizable, there are in every water fishes which, on account of their small size, rarity, retiring habits, or close similarity to other fishes, are unknown."
—Hugh M. Scott, *The Official Handbook for Boys,
Boy Scouts of America*, 1922

Chapter 7. Key to Common Fishes of the Region

During my short career as a fish checker, an angler bragged that he knew what Arctic grayling looked like because he caught the last one in the state of Washington. Several years later, another angler claimed to have recaptured a smallmouth bass that I had tagged for research purposes. Both anglers confused their target species with a northern pikeminnow. The lesson is that unless you know what to look for or have years of experience, many fishes look similar. Being able to know one species from another is important for more reasons than culinary pursuit. In the case of salmon versus steelhead, knowing the difference might prevent you from getting a ticket.

Knowledge of various body parts of a fish and how to make certain counts and measurements is a prerequisite to using the key provided in this chapter. It is most helpful to review all terms and definitions and study important features for major types of fishes before attempting to identify a specimen. The glossary of common taxonomic terms, in addition to pictures located throughout the key, also will help in distinguishing one group of fishes from another. Please review the information provided in chapter 6 (in particular, refer to Figures 6.1, 6.2, 6.3, 6.4 and 6.9) when identifying a fish.

In some ways, identifying an unknown fish is like solving a mystery. It works best if you work through the process step-by-step to identify all possible clues before making an identification. After a preliminary identification of the fish is made, refer to the more complete description in chapter 8 to confirm your choice and to find more information about a particular species. Multiple clues may be required before correct identification is possible.

This key is arranged in two sections. The first is a key to families. In some cases, only one species of fish from that family is found in the Columbia Basin. This situation makes species identification fairly easy. The second section is organized by family with a key provided to allow identification to individual species from more diverse families of fishes. In both sections, a dichotomous arrangement is used. This arrangement provides a choice between a set of two, alternate and typically contrasting characters that are designated by either "a" or "b." You must select the correct statement and continue in the key as indicated to the next pair of statements or to the name of the family to which the specimen belongs.

Most features described in this book are those of adult fish. Additional information on distinctive features of juvenile life stages is provided where it is important for their identification. Note that color, body proportions and other features of fishes may change according to age, sex, stage of reproductive cycle, time of year and geographic region. When in doubt, rely on features that can be counted.

Geographically, the species described occur in an area covered by three states – roughly the Spokane River basin in northeast Washington downstream to the Willamette River, Oregon, and upstream to where the Clearwater River merges with the Snake River at Lewiston, Idaho. The Columbia Basin is bound by the Cascade Mountains to the west, Okanogan Highlands to the north and Blue Mountains to the south and east. Descriptions of fishes may not be useful outside of this region.

Several regional texts were consulted to develop this key, including Schultz (1936), Carl, Clemens and Lindsey (1973), Simpson and Wallace (1982), Bond (1994) and Wydoski and Whitney (2003). Common and scientific names of the families and species used are those recommended in the American Fisheries Society Special Publication 29, "Common and Scientific Names of Fishes from the United States, Canada, and Mexico," (Nelson and six coauthors, 2004). Readers can refer to Appendix A for a complete checklist of fishes found within the region and for an indication of whether they are common or rare.

Do not fear a key. With practice, and as terms become more familiar, identifying most fishes is easy. I provide both common and scientific names of all fishes to help in the process. If all else fails, look at the color photos provided for all but the least common species.

Section 1. Key to Families

All line drawings in the Key to Families are from C.E. Bond, *Keys to Oregon Fishes*, Corvallis, Oregon, 1994.

1a. Has no paired fins, jaws or scales; mouth is a circular, suctorial "sucking" disc; a series of seven, round gill openings are present on each side of the pharyngeal or head region.

Lampreys – Family Petromyzontidae, page 94

1b. Paired fins and jaws are present. There is a single gill opening on each side. See 2.
2a. Upper lobe of the caudal or tail fin is much longer than the lower, or "heterocercal;" the side of the body has a series of bony plates, or scutes; the hard, cartilagenous snout narrows into a rostrum; four barbels are present in advance of an inferior or down-turned mouth.

Sturgeons – Family Acipenseridae, page 94

2b. Caudal fin is not heterocercal, i.e., both lobes are nearly equal in length; mouth is forward or terminal. See 3.
3a. An adipose fin is present. See 4.
3b. Has no adipose fin. See 7.
4a. Scales are absent from body; several pairs of barbels are present near the mouth.

Catfishes – Family Ictaluridae, page 95

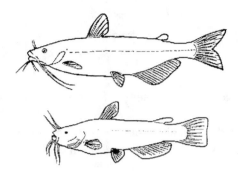

4b. Scales are present; no barbels near the mouth. See 5.
5a. Sharp spines are present in dorsal, anal and pelvic fins; scales are ctenoid; has an adipose fin.

Trout-perches – Family Percopsidae, page 95

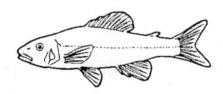

5b. No spines on fins; scales are cycloid. See 6.
6a. No accessory pelvic appendage; mouth moderately large; no spotting on body.

Smelts – Family Osmeridae, page 96

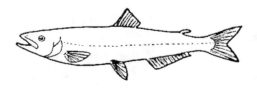

6b. Accessory pelvic appendage present; fins composed of soft rays only; spotting or parr marks (see Figure 6.1) usually present, particularly for juvenile life stage.

Trout, Salmon, Chars and Whitefishes – Family Salmonidae, page 96

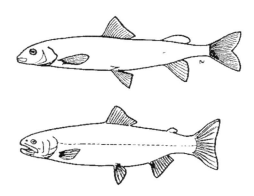

7a. Pelvic fins are slightly forward of the dorsal fin base; mouth may have teeth. See 8.
7b. Pelvic fins are abdominal or behind the front edge of the dorsal fin; mouth lacks teeth. See 14.
8a. A single "beatnik-like" barbel is present on the point of the lower jaw; with two dorsal fins, the first one is short, the second dorsal fin reaches about half the length of the back; has an eel-shaped body; pelvic fin is placed forward (thoracic); caudal fin is rounded.

Freshwater Cod or Burbot – Family Gadidae, page 100

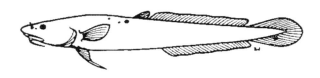

8b. No barbel is present on the lower jaw or chin. See 9.

9a. Head is flattened (i.e., duckbill-like) and wide with scales on side; forked tail.

Pikes – Family Esocidae, page 100

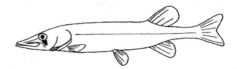

9b. Head not flattened and without an elongate snout. See 10.
10a. Caudal fin is rounded or truncated; has no anal fin spines. See 11.
10b. Caudal fin is deeply indented; anal fin has spines on the leading edge; mouth has teeth. See 13.
11a. Has two dorsal fins that may be joined. Lacks scales on the body, however often has minute prickles; eyes are placed close together high on head; dorsal spines are flexible. Pectoral fins are large and conspicuous. Body is cylindrical in shape.

Sculpins – Family Cottidae, page 100

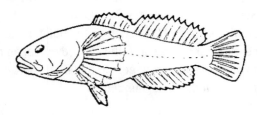

11b. Single small dorsal fin; has noticeable scales; anal fin is slightly in advance or below the dorsal fin. Premaxillaries are protractile with a groove separating the top of the upper lip. Small fishes rarely more than 3 to 4 inches long. See 12.
12a. Origin of dorsal fin posterior to the origin of anal fin. Caudal fin is rounded; males with anal fin modified into a slender, intromittent organ or "gonopodium."

Live-bearers – Family Poeciliidae, page 101

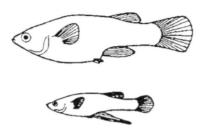

12b. Origin of dorsal fin anterior to origin of anal fin. Usually with several, dark vertical bars along the side of the body.

Killifish – Family Cyprinodontidae, page 102

13a. Has two separate dorsal fins; sides are yellowish; there is a sharp spine on the gill cover, or opercle, and/or canine teeth are present.

Perches – Family Percidae, page 102

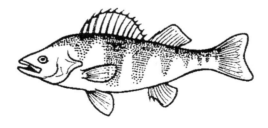

13b. The dorsal fin is single or has a deep notch near the juncture of the spinous (first) and soft (second) portions; no spine is present on the opercle, or gill cover; anal fin has fewer than 20 soft rays.

Sunfishes and bass – Family Centrarchidae, page 102

14a. The lower gill membranes or branchiostegals are free from the isthmus (gill openings are wide; refer to Figure 6.12). See 15.

14b. Gill membranes are attached to the isthmus (gill openings are narrow). See 16.

15a. Body is rounded. Two prominent spines are present in front of the dorsal fin and are not connected to it; a third spine can be found at the front edge of the dorsal fin; small, bony plates, or scutes, are on the sides. Rarely more than 3 inches in length.

Sticklebacks – Family Gasterosteidae, page 103

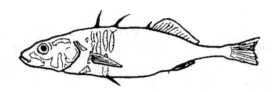

15b. Body is compressed laterally. Caudal fin is deeply forked. Single dorsal fin; no lateral line of sensory pores along the side; midline of the belly has a bony, serrated ridge, often having a row of spots in front of the pectoral fins.

Herrings – Family Clupeidae, page 103

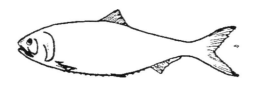

16a. Anal fin is set back from the anterior edge of the dorsal fin; no serrated spinelike rays are present at the anterior of dorsal and anal fins; the mouth is down-turned, or inferior; has generally thick lips with small nubs, or papillae. Has 20 or more pharyngeal teeth in a row (refer to Figure 6.7).

Suckers – Family Catostomidae, page 103

16b. Anal fin origin is directly below or slightly in advance of the back edge of the dorsal fin. May have spines or spine-like rays in the anterior dorsal or anal fins. May have small barbels on the corner of the mouth. Never with more than six pharyngeal teeth in a row (refer to Figure 6.7).

Minnows and Carps – Family Cyprinidae, page 105

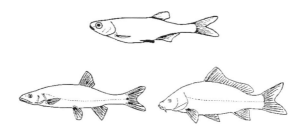

Section 2. Key to Individual Species

This section is a key to 17 different families of fishes and the most commonly encountered species in the Columbia Basin. The arrangement is sequential following the order in the family key.

Lampreys – Family Petromyzontidae

1a. Eyes present; mouth not hooded, a "buccal" funnel is evident; teeth are present. See 2.
1b. No eyes are evident; mouth covered with a hood (larval, or ammocoete). This life stage is very difficult to identify species.
2a. Has a series of small teeth in the posterior portion of its oral disc; supraoral lamina with three cusps (refer to Figure 7.1). Adults are usually 18 to 36 inches long.
Pacific lamprey, *Lampetra tridentata*

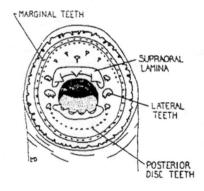

Figure 7.1. Teeth in the sucking mouth of Pacific lamprey (from C.E. Bond, *Keys to Oregon Fishes*, Corvallis, Oregon, 1994)

2b. Teeth are dull; the adult form is usually less than 8 inches in length; dorsal fins are separated at the base.
Western brook lamprey, *Lampetra richardsoni*

Sturgeons – Family Acipenseridae

1a. Lateral scutes range from 38 to 48; barbels are closer to the end of the

snout than the mouth; snout is short and rounded; body color is gray.
White sturgeon, *Acipenser transmontanus*

1b. Lateral scutes range from 23 to 30; barbels are closer to the mouth than the snout; snout is long and narrow; body color is greenish.
Green sturgeon, *Acipenser medirostris*

Catfishes – Family Ictaluridae

1a. Adipose fin is joined to the front edge of the caudal fin. Less than 6 inches long.
Tadpole madtom, *Noturus gyrinus*

1b. Adipose fin is separated from caudal fin. See 2.
2a. Caudal fin is deeply forked; anal fin has more than 25 rays.
Channel catfish, *Ictalurus punctatus*

2b. Caudal fin is rounded, or emarginate. See 3, "bullheads."
3a. No barbs are present on the posterior edge of the pectoral spine. Fin membranes are jet black; mental (chin) barbels are gray to black.
Black bullhead, *Ameiurus melas*

3b. Short barbs are present on posterior edge of pectoral spine. Color of the fin membranes is the same (i.e., does not contrast with) the fin rays. See 4.
4a. Mental or chin barbels are white; anal fin rays range from 24 to 27.
Yellow bullhead, *Ameirus natalis*

4b. Mental or chin barbels are gray to black at tips; anal fin rays range from 17 to 24.
Brown bullhead, *Ameirus nebulosus*

Trout-perches – Family Percopsidae

There is one member of this family in the Columbia Basin.

Sand roller, *Percopsis transmontanus*

Smelts – Family Osmeridae

There is one member of this family in the Columbia Basin.

Eulachon, *Thaleichthys pacificus*

Salmon, Trout, Chars and Whitefishes – Family Salmonidae

1a. Scales are relatively large, fewer than 100 are present on the lateral line; mouth is small; teeth are poorly developed or absent; no spotting is evident in adults. See 2, "whitefishes."
1b. Scales are small, greater than 100 on lateral line; the body of most have noticeable spots. See 3.
2a. Mouth is small and pointed; have a single flap between the nostrils (refer to Figure 7.2). Body is cylindrical in shape.
Mountain whitefish, *Prosopium williamsoni*

2b. Mouth is larger, maxillary reaches to the front edge of the eye; have a double flap between the nostrils. Body is deep relative to width.
Lake whitefish, *Coregonus clupeaformis*

3a. Body with light spots on a darker background; teeth are present only on the head of the vomer (refer to Figure 7.3). Mouth is relatively large. See 4, "chars."
3b. Body with dark spots on a lighter background; if spots are lacking, anal rays are greater than 13; teeth are present on head and shaft of vomer (Figure 7.3). See 6, "Trout and Salmon."
4a. Back and dorsal fin have wavy marks (vermiculations); body usually has crimson spots surrounded by blue halos; anterior edge of lower (anal and pelvic) fins has a white edge bordered by a black stripe.
Brook trout, *Salvelinus fontinalis*

4b. Marks on dorsal fin and back do not form vermiculations. White leading edges of lower fins lack a black border. See 5.
5a. Caudal fin is deeply forked (i.e., shortest ray is less than half of the length of the longest ray). The body has irregular white or gray spots.
Lake trout, *Salvelinus namaycush*

5b. Caudal fin is only slightly forked (i.e., shortest ray is greater than half the longest ray). Back and sides of body are greenish and covered with small creamy to crimson-colored spots.

Bull trout, *S. confluentus*

6a. Interior of mouth is white; less than 13 anal rays. See 7, "trouts."
6b. Interior of mouth is blackish in adults; more than 13 anal rays. See 9, "salmons."
7a. Basibranchial (hyoid) teeth are present behind the tongue (refer to Figure 7.3); usually with pronounced red-orange "slash" marks present under each side of lower jaw; spots on body are usually large, round and distinct; inland forms with no or minute spots on head; head is long, mouth is large, i.e., maxillary usually reaches to the hind margin of the eye.

Cutthroat trout, *Oncorhynchus clarki*

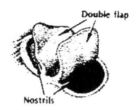

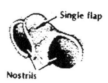

Figure 7.2 Nostril flap characteristics for mountain and lake whitefishes (from C.J.D Brown, Fishes of Montana, Bozeman, Montana, 1971).

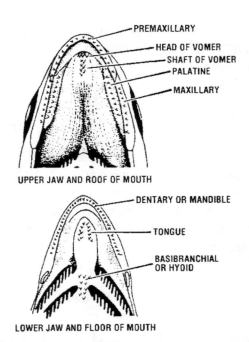

Figure 7.3 Teeth in the mouth of char, trout and salmon (from R.S. Wydoski and R.R. Whitney, *Inland Fishes of Washington*, Seattle, 2003

    7b. Basibranchial teeth are absent; red slash marks under the lower jaw are usually absent; often with a distinct red band along the lateral line. See 8.
    8a. Caudal or tail fin usually lacks spots; red spots may be present on the body, with halos or spots may be C- or X-shaped; usually have eight to nine anal rays; back and sides are typically yellowish-brown. Young have an orange adipose fin.
Brown trout, *Salmo trutta*

    8b. Spotting on caudal fin and top of head is usually profuse; no red spots on the body; often have a red or rosy streak along their sides, particularly mature adults; usually have 10 to 12 anal fin rays.
Rainbow trout and steelhead, *Oncorhynchus mykiss*

    9a. No distinct black spots on back or caudal fin. May have fine speckling. See 10.
    9b. Distinct black spotting on back and caudal fin; usually less than 30 gill rakers on first arch; young with vertical parr marks extending well below lateral line. See 11.

10a. Has 30 or more slender gill rakers on the first branchial arch (refer to Figure 6.11); 95 or fewer pyloric caeca (refer to Figure 6.10); caudal peduncle is slender; young have small irregular parr marks located primarily above the lateral line.
Sockeye salmon (anadromous or sea-going form) and kokanee (landlocked form), *Oncorhynchus nerka*

10b. Gill rakers on first arch range from 19 to 26 and are short, stout and far apart. Pyloric caeca range from 140 to 186.
Chum salmon, *Oncorhynchus keta*

11a. Have large black spots on the back and caudal fin (some are as large as the eye). Scales are very small, ranging from 169 to 229 in the first row above the lateral line.
Pink salmon, *Oncorhynchus gorbuscha*

11b. Small black spots are present on the back and caudal fin; less than 154 scales in the first row above the lateral line. See 12.
12a. Teeth of adult salmon with a white gum line; pyloric caeca range from 45 to 85 (refer to Figure 6.10). Tail is spotted on upper fin lobe only. Young salmon have parr marks bisected by the lateral line and narrower than the light areas between (Figure 7.4). In addition, the first few rays of the anal fin are elongated and tipped with white.
Coho salmon, *Oncorhynchus kisutch*

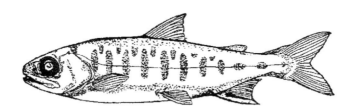

Figure 7.4. Juvenile coho salmon showing parr marks and elongated anal fin (from C.E. Bond, *Keys to Oregon Fishes*, Corvallis, Oregon, 1994)

12b. Teeth of adults are set in a dark gum line; typically have small profuse spotting present in both lobes of the caudal fin; have more than 140 pyloric caeca (refer to Figure 6.9). Young have parr marks bisected by the

lateral line and usually wider than the light areas in between.
Chinook salmon, *Oncorhynchus tshawytscha*

Cods – Family Gadidae

There is only one member of this family in the Columbia Basin.

Burbot or freshwater ling, *Lota lota*

Pikes – Family Esocidae

    1a. Cheek and opercle are both completely covered with scales; four sensory pores on each side of the lower jaw; usually with 11 to 12 branchiostegal rays (refer to Figure 6.13) along the lower edge of the gill cover. Rarely more than 10 inches in length.
Grass pickerel, *Esox americanus*

    1b. Scales absent from most of the opercle; five sensory pores on each side of the lower jaw; usually with 14 to 16 branchiostegal rays (refer to Figure 6.13); sides of body with light horizontal markings on a dark background.
Northern pike, *Esox lucius*

Sculpins – Family Cottidae

    1a. Second dorsal fin is quite long with more than 19 rays; anal fin is also relatively long with more than 16 rays; dorsal fins are conjoined, usually to one-third the height of first soft ray; body is well covered with tiny prickles (can be felt by rubbing your fingers across the sides).
Prickly sculpin, *Cottus asper*

    1b. Anal fin is relatively short: less than 12 rays; dorsal fins are well-separated to base. See 2.
    2a. Head is large, usually more than one-third standard length; spines along the front edge of the gill cover (pre-opercular) usually number three to four; palatine teeth (refer to Figure 7.5) are absent. See 3.

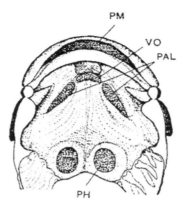

Figure 7.5. Location of teeth in the roof of a sculpin mouth (from C.E. Bond, *Keys to Oregon Fishes*, Corvallis, Oregon, 1994)

2b. Palatine teeth are absent. See 4.

3a. Caudal peduncle is slender; lateral line is complete; specimens usually with two dark bars that slant forward under the second dorsal fin; has two or four pre-opercular spines.
Torrent sculpin, *Cottus rhotheus*

3b. Caudal fin depth is approximately one-fourth the head length; spinous (first) dorsal has two dark blotches, one on the front edge and one on the back edge; breeding males are very dark and have an orange margin on the front of the first dorsal fin.
Mottled sculpin, *Cottus bairdi*

4a. Median chin pore is absent; lateral complex line is incomplete; have 11 to 13 anal rays and one or two pre-opercular spines.
Pauite sculpin, *Cottus beldingi*

4b. A median chin pore is usually present; typically with two pre-opercular spines; the body is short and blunt.
Margined sculpin, *Cottus marginatus*

Live-bearers – Family Poeciliidae

1a. Origin of the dorsal fin is far behind the origin of the anal fin. Male has a long anal fin (gonopodium).

Mosquitofish, *Gambusia affinis*

    1b. Origin of the dorsal fin is even with the dorsal fin origin; male has a short anal fin.
Guppy, *Poecilia reticulata*

Killifishes – Family Cyprinidontidae

  There is one member of this family in the Columbia Basin.

Banded killifish, *Fundulus diaphanus*

Perches – Family Percidae

    1a. Body is somewhat compressed; has a distinct pattern of dark vertical bars along the sides; no canine teeth are present in the mouth; has seven to nine anal soft rays.
Yellow perch, *Perca flavescens*

    1b. Body is more cylindrical in shape; coloration is mottled, without a distinct pattern of dark vertical bars; large, sharp, "canine-like" teeth are present in the mouth; anal soft rays are greater than or equal to 12.
Walleye, *Sander vitreus*

Bass and Sunfishes – Family Centrarchidae

    1a. Anal fin length is equal to the length of the dorsal fin base; has five or more anal spines. See 2.
    1b. Anal fin length is approximately one-half of the dorsal fin; has three anal spines. See 3.
    2a. Length of the dorsal fin base is less than the distance from origin of dorsal fin to the eye; has five to six dorsal spines.
White crappie, *Pomoxis annularis*

    2b. Length of the dorsal fin base is equal to or more than distance from the origin of the dorsal fin to the eye; has seven to eight dorsal spines.
Black crappie, *Pomoxis nigromaculatus*

    3a. Mouth is relatively small, maxillary or lower jawbone barely extends to the front edge of the eye; supramaxilla are small or absent; pectoral fins are long and pointed. See 4.

3b. Mouth is large, maxillary extends at least to the middle of the eye; supramaxilla is present; pectoral fins are rounded. See 5.

4a. Gill rakers are long and slender, their length is greater than the diameter of pupil; lack a red spot on the opercle, or gill cover flap; dark blotch is present on the posterior of the dorsal fin base; back edge of the opercle is flexible.

Bluegill, *Lepomis macrochirus*

4b. Gill rakers are stuffy, length less than diameter of the pupil; opercle flap has no red or orange spot; opercle is stiff to the margin.

Pumpkinseed, *Lepomis gibbosus*

5a. Upper jaw extends well beyond the posterior edge of the eye; a deep notch is present between the first (spinous) and second (soft) dorsal fins; a thick dark lateral line is usually present along the side; has less than 69 scales along the lateral line.

Largemouth bass, *Micropterus salmoides*

5b. Upper jaw does not extend beyond the posterior margin of the eye; shallow notch is present between the spinous and soft dorsal rays; the shortest dorsal spine is longer than one-half the length of the longest spine; vertical banding occurs along the sides of the body; has more than 68 lateral line scales.

Smallmouth bass, *Micropterus dolomieu*

Sticklebacks – Family Gasterosteidae

There is only one member of this family in the Columbia Basin.

Three-spine stickleback, *Gasterosteus aculeatus*

Herrings – Family Clupeidae

There is only one member of this family in the Columbia Basin.

American shad, *Alosa sapidissima*

Suckers – Family Catostomidae

1a. The median notch that separates the lobes of the lower lip is shallow, leaving three to five rows of papillae, or "nubs," between the notch and the edge of the lower jaw; cartilaginous biting "sheath" on the lower jaw is well-developed and truncated; there is a prominent notch at the side of the mouth or juncture of upper and lower lip. Adults are usually less than 10 inches in length.
Mountain sucker, *Catostomus platyrhynchus*

1b. The notch separating the lobes of the lower lip is deep, leaving three or fewer rows of papillae between it and lower jaw (refer to Figure 7.6). Cartilaginous sheath of lower jaw is rounded; lower lip notches are either weak or absent. See 2.

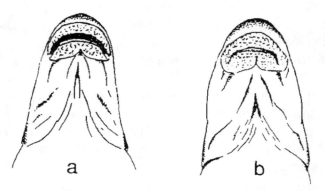

Figure 7.6 Lower lip and mouth of bridgelip sucker and largescale sucker (author figure)

2a. Scales on the lateral line are usually less than 80; dorsal fin rays range from 13 to 15; the caudal peduncle is slender, its depth is less than one-half the length of the dorsal fin base; median notch separating lower lobe of lip is deep, usually with one or no rows of papillae present; the body color is brown with a yellow tinge.
Largescale sucker, *Catostomus macrocheilus*

2b. Scales on the lateral line are usually greater than 80; dorsal rays range from nine to 12. See 3.

3a. Scales on the lateral line are usually greater than 85; caudal peduncle depth is about one-half of the length of the dorsal fin base; dorsal fin rays

range from 11 to 13; the median notch separating the lower lip is shallow with two to three rows of papillae present; the body color is typically greenish-brown.
Bridgelip sucker, *Catostomus columbianus*

3b. The lower lip is completely cleft in its midline with only one row of papillae; the mouth is conspicuously overhung by the snout; has nine to 11 dorsal fin rays.
Longnose sucker, *Catostomus catostomus*

Minnows – Family Cyprinidae

1a. The caudal fin is squared off or truncated; body is robust; has more than 100 scales in lateral line.
Tench, *Tinca tinca*

1b. The caudal fin is forked. See 2.
2a. Dorsal and anal fins have no spines. See 4.
2b. A spine, usually serrated, or "saw-toothed," is present in front of both the dorsal and anal fins. See 3.
3a. Has two pairs of barbels on the upper jaw; 21 to 27 gill rakers on first arch.
Carp, *Cyprinus carpio*

3b. Has no barbels in the corner of the mouth; 37 to 43 gill rakers on first arch.
Goldfish, *Carassius auratus*

4a. Lower jaw has a broad, straight-edged horny plate (refer to Figure 7.7).
Chiselmouth, *Acrocheilus alutaceus*

Figure 7.7. Straight-edged lower jaw of a chiselmouth (from C.E. Bond, *Keys to Oregon Fishes*, Corvallis, Oregon, 1994)

4b. Lower jaw rounded or without a straight-edged horny plate. See 5.
5a. Anal fin is long, usually with more than 15 rays; body is deep and strongly compressed.
Redside shiner, *Richardsonius balteatus*

5b. Anal fin has less than 10 rays; body is not deep or compressed. See 6.
6a. Mouth is distinctly inferior, or down-turned (refer to Figure 6.6). See 7.
6b. Mouth is not inferior. See 9.
7a. Premaxillaries are not protractile; a frenum, or bridge, connects the upper lip with the snout (refer to Figure 7.8 B).
Longnose dace, *Rhinichthys cataractae*

7b. Premaxillaries cannot be separated from the snout (protractile) i.e., the upper lip is separated from the snout by a narrow groove or is protractile (refer to Figure 7.8 A). See 8.
8a. Scales with radii (Figure 6.8) present in all fields.
Speckled dace, *Rhinichthys osculus* complex (includes *C. umatilla*)

8b. Scales with radii absent from basal or embedded field of scale. Fin rays may be orangish in mature males.
Leopard dace, *Rhinichthys falcatus*

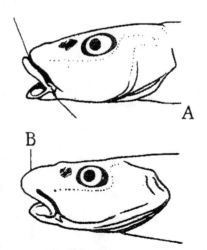

Figure 7.8 A and B. Comparison of two types of premaxillaries (from C.E. Bond, *Keys to Oregon Fishes*, Corvallis, Oregon, 1994)

9a. Body is trout-like but yellowish in color; head is relatively long, ranging from 22 to 23 percent of the total length; mouth is large, extends at least to front margin of eye; young less than 4 inches long have a black spot at the base of the caudal fin.
Northern pikeminnow, *Ptychocheilus oregonensis*

9b. Head short, mouth does not extend beyond the front margin of eye. See 10.
10a. Head length is less than 20 percent of total length; snout slightly overhangs mouth; a small barbel or "nub" is present at corners of the jaw; front of the dorsal fin is forward of or opposite the front of the pelvic fin base.
Peamouth chub, *Mylocheilus caurinus*

10b. Barbels are absent from the corner of the mouth. See 11.
11a. Lateral line is incomplete; mouth is small and oblique in shape; the first dorsal fin ray is blunt and thickened; scales in front of the dorsal fin are crowded.
Fathead minnow, *Pimephales promelas*

11b. Lateral line is complete; mouth moderate in size; scales in front of the dorsal fin are not notably crowded; less than 65 lateral line scales.
Tui chub, *Gila bicolor*

•••

Each species is a world unto itself. It is a unique part of Nature.
—E.O. Wilson, *The Creation*, 2006

Chapter 8. Biology of Columbia Basin Fishes

This chapter includes biological descriptions of more than 60 species of fishes from 17 families. Individual species accounts were largely summarized from information found in books, published reports and journal articles listed in the reference section at the end of this chapter. Please refer to these references for more detail on species of interest.

The chapter is organized by family, or the taxonomic grouping above genus. The amount of detail provided for each species depends on their relative abundance, economic importance and public interest. Distinguishing characteristics are included to assist in species identification, but don't use this feature as an excuse not to use the key provided in chapter 7. The general biological description of each species includes facts on their distribution and habitat use, spawning, feeding, age and growth. For more important sport fishes, I include fishing facts and local lore.

Lampreys – Family Petromyzontidae

Lampreys are an ancient form of fishes that are cartilaginous, highly elongated and smooth bodied. They are unique among all other local fishes in lacking jaws, ribs and paired fins. The mouth of an adult lamprey is surrounded by a circular sucking disk and has horny teeth. Lampreys have a single median nostril on the top of their head and a series of seven circular gill ports on each side of the body near the head. Some might consider them ugly.

Two species of lampreys are commonly encountered in the Columbia River drainage, one anadromous and the other resident. A third species, the river lamprey (*Lampetra ayresi*), may also be present, but its distribution and population status is poorly documented. The river lamprey is unique because it feeds on other fish, is predatory rather than parasitic.

Pacific lamprey, *Lampetra tridentata* (native). Other common names include three-toothed lamprey.

Distinguishing Characteristics
Adult Pacific lamprey are 12 to 36 inches in length. They have sharp teeth, a supra-oral lamina with three cusps, and the posterior teeth are mostly continuous with lateral teeth. These unusual fish reach lengths of up to 3 feet and are often referred

to as "eels." However, true eels have a bony skeleton and are an East Coast species that migrate downstream to the Atlantic Ocean as adults.

Life History and Behavior

Pacific lampreys are found in coastal streams from Southern California to the Gulf of Alaska. Columbia River populations have declined significantly during the latter part of the 20th century. Numbers of adult Pacific lampreys migrating over Bonneville Dam have declined from 350,000 in the 1960s to 22,000 in 1997. After 1969, the number of Pacific lampreys passing Rock Island Dam declined precipitously coincident with inundation of spawning habitat by Rocky Reach and Wells Dam. A similar pattern of decline was observed in the lower Snake River after completion of the Hells Canyon complex and the four lower Snake River dams.

Current viable populations in the Columbia Basin occur in the Tucannon, Umatilla, John Day, Deschutes and Willamette rivers. There is limited spawning in the Hanford Reach of the Columbia River. Factors contributing to the decline of Pacific lampreys include habitat degradation, reduced access to spawning habitat, loss to predators, migration blockage and entrainment at dams and water diversion structures. Pacific lamprey are considered a Washington State Species of Concern. It's only a matter of time before Columbia River populations may be listed under the Endangered Species Act.

Adult lampreys enter freshwater from May to September, then "hold over" prior to spawning the following March or April. Both sexes build a nest in sandy gravel using body vibrations or by moving rocks with their suctorial disc. When the nest is ready, the female attaches to a rock while the male goes through courtship display. Eggs hatch in two to three weeks. After hatching, their larvae, or "ammocoetes," burrow into the sand and gravel where they remain for five to seven years. Larvae feed on microscopic algae. During this time, Pacific lampreys have an oral hood, lack teeth and the eyes are underdeveloped.

Juvenile lampreys resemble small garter snakes when they emerge from their burrows and swim to the Pacific Ocean. They become parasitic only after metamorphosing into a young adult. When these rubbery hitchhikers attach to the body of fish via their suckerlike mouth, a toothed tongue rasps a small hole into the host's body, sucking body fluids and blood for nourishment. An anticoagulant fluid is produced to prevent the host's blood from clotting. Host fish are weakened by such attacks but may survive. Lamprey teeth marks also have been found in migrating whales, although some scars indicated that their mammal hosts merely served a transport function.

Adult Pacific lamprey use a combination of maneuvers to navigate upstream past dams and other barriers. If water velocities are high, they attach to objects, rest, then swim in short bursts. Lamprey can also use their tails as an appendage to help them "flip-flop" or "corkscrew" over vertical obstacles, including steep waterfalls. The U.S. Army Corps of Engineers has funded research to improve the passage of adult lampreys past main stem dams and to improve conditions for downstream-migrating juvenile lamprey that encounter turbine intake screens.

Historically, adult lampreys were used as coyote bait by Northwest fur trappers. Ichthyologists Charles Gilbert and Barton Evermann reported in 1893 that lamprey were caught by fish wheels on the lower Snake and Columbia rivers in such numbers as to "fill the boat."

Until the 1970s, tribal fishers netted lamprey at Bonneville Dam. Willamette Falls is currently the largest lamprey fishery in the Columbia River system. Numbers there were high enough to support a commercial catch in the 1940s. Adult lampreys are gathered from rocks at Willamette Falls during their upstream migration interval in the spring. Since 2000, the commercial harvest has been restricted because of concerns over a declining population.

Several Indian tribes still harvest adult lamprey for food. It has been reported that enjoyment of the meat is an acquired taste as lampreys are very oily. Elsewhere, adult lampreys are widely used as bait for white sturgeon. Ammocoetes have been used as bait for bass. This practice is illegal in Washington if fish are alive.

Western brook lamprey, *Lampetra richardsoni* (native)

Distinguishing Characteristics
The adult brook lamprey is usually less than 7 inches in length and has dull, non-functional teeth. Larvae lack pigment in the membraneous tip of the caudal fin.

Life History and Behavior
Western brook lamprey are the only member of this interesting group of fishes that spends its entire life in freshwater. Spawning takes place in the spring. Nests are usually constructed among small rocks mixed with sand at the head of a riffle. The nest may be only 2 inches deep and 4 to 5 inches in diameter. Like their larger

cousin, brook lamprey move gravel with body vibrations and their mouths. During spawning, the female attaches to a stone. The male fastens himself to the female and twines his body around hers to ensure that eggs and sperm are released simultaneously.

Larvae brook lamprey burrow in bottom silt of back eddies and feed on microscopic material filtered from the water. After four to six years, they transform to the adult stage. Adults do not feed; their only function is to reproduce.

Brook lamprey ammocoetes and transformed adults were at one time gathered extensively for bait in Washington. They have been widely used to angle for bass and sturgeon. They have no value as a food fish because of their small size. Brook lamprey are listed as a Washington State Species of Concern.

Sturgeons – Family Acipenseridae

Sturgeons are characterized by having a long body with five rows of sharp, bony plates or scutes along their sides and dorsal ridge. Their caudal fin is heterocercal, or asymmetrical, with the upper fin lobe being longer than the lower. The mouth is down-turned (inferior) and it elongates to allow them to suck food off the stream bottom like a vacuum cleaner. Sturgeons have four whisker-like barbels on the lower surface of the snout to help them detect prey. Worldwide, sturgeons are in need of effective conservation due to overexploitation by commercial harvest and loss of critical habitats, such as flowing water. Two species of sturgeons occur in the Columbia Basin.

White sturgeon, *Acipenser transmontanus* (native). Other common names include Pacific sturgeon, Oregon sturgeon and Columbia sturgeon.

The white sturgeon is the largest freshwater fish in North America and the most common of the two species found in the Columbia River. Specimens of up to 20 feet long and 1,800 pounds have been reported from British Columbia. By 1900, populations were decimated in the Columbia River due to overharvest. Stocks rebounded in the lower Columbia River after the 6-foot maximum size limit was enacted in 1950. The regulation effectively protected fish once they reached sexual maturity.

White sturgeon populations are now landlocked between most hydroelectric projects because adults can't easily navigate fish ladders designed mainly for upstream passage of salmon and steelhead. Low numbers may pass through navigation locks. There is some juvenile movement downstream past dams. Because adults can no longer migrate freely throughout the Columbia and Snake rivers, upstream populations are isolated and depressed in number. Only remnant populations occur upstream of Priest Rapids Dam in the Columbia River and in the Hells Canyon Reach of the Snake River.

Distinguishing Characteristics

White sturgeons are grayish on top with a white belly. They have a short, rounded snout with four barbels, or "whiskers," that are closer to the end of the snout than to the mouth. White sturgeons have 38 to 48 scutes or hard bony plates along each side and four to eight scutes between the pelvic and anal fins.

Life History and Behavior

White sturgeons are usually found in the deepest holes of large rivers. Those in the Hanford Reach of the Columbia River seek depths to 60 feet. The largest populations are in the lower Columbia River downstream of Bonneville Dam where up to 1 million sturgeons may reside. Many of these fish migrate to the Pacific Ocean and back. Lower Columbia River reservoir populations ranged from 30,000 to 80,000 sturgeons based on surveys conducted in the 1990s. In the free-flowing Hanford Reach, white sturgeons occupy deep holes in the winter and are inactive until water temperatures approach 50 F to 55 F in the spring. Radio-tagging studies showed that smaller sturgeons tended to move downstream and larger fish upstream as water warmed. Movement ceased when temperatures declined to 50 F in the fall. During the summer, sturgeons may move from cool, deep areas before sunrise and to warmer, shallow water after sunset.

White sturgeons must have fast-flowing water to reproduce, such as that found in the Hanford Reach and tailrace areas immediately downstream of main stem dams. Spawning occurs from April to July at water temperatures between 48 F and 63 F. Not all white sturgeons will spawn in a given year. Mature white sturgeons broadcast as many as a million or more eggs that sink and attach to substrate. Eggs hatch in about a week at 59 F. The habits and distribution of young-of-the-year white sturgeons are elusive.

White sturgeons grow slowly and live a long time. Males generally mature at 4 feet and 10 years of age and females at 6 feet and 15 years. White sturgeons as old as 104 years have been identified from the Columbia River based on analysis of sections taken from pectoral fin rays.

White sturgeons are mainly bottom feeders and have a good sense of smell. They eat a wide variety of food including insect larvae, amphipods, clams and fishes such as sucker, American shad and spawned-out salmon. Fishermen take advantage of their behavior by fishing on the bottom with large baits that "milk" scent.

In the Columbia River, recreational anglers are limited to keeping white sturgeons within a mid-range size or "slot" length. This regulation protects both smaller, immature fish and those old enough to reproduce. The size limit for white sturgeon that can be kept in the Mid-Columbia region is from 48 inches to 60 inches in total length. Larger fish are often caught but must be released unharmed. No sight is more spectacular than that of an 8-foot-long sturgeon going topwater. Popular bait includes American shad, Pacific lamprey and salmon "bellies." The primary recreational fishery upstream of Bonneville Dam is in the three-pool areas of Zone 6, in the Hanford Reach and upstream of Grand Coulee Dam in Lake Roosevelt. Sturgeon fishing in the Snake River is limited to a catch-and-release fishery in the Hells Canyon Reach.

Green sturgeon, *Acipenser medirostris* (native)

Green sturgeons are the smaller of the two species. They frequent coastal waters and the lower reach of the Columbia River downstream of Bonneville Dam but are rarely seen.

Distinguishing Characteristics
The snout is long and narrow and barbels are closer to the mouth than the tip of the snout. It has eight to 11 dorsal scutes and 23 to 30 lateral scutes. The body and head are dark green to olive green in color. They may have a greenish stripe between the lateral and ventral row of scutes.

Life History and Behavior
Green sturgeons are thought to migrate from the Pacific Ocean in late summer and early fall into the lower Columbia River. Little is known of their life history. They may spawn in May to June, similar to white sturgeons. They are mainly bottom feeders, eating invertebrates and fishes such as eulachon. The maximum size reported for green sturgeons is 7 feet long and 350 pounds.

The flesh of green sturgeons is dark, has a disagreeable taste and unpleasant odor. Small numbers are harvested each year in the commercial gill net fishery in the lower 40 miles of the Columbia River. Recreational harvest is usually less than

500 fish annually.

Herrings – Family Clupeidae

A single species from this family, American shad, is present in the Columbia Basin. Although shad are revered by anglers in the eastern part of the United States, in the salmon-centric Pacific Northwest, they are often viewed as a pest. Shad often migrate in such large numbers that they often prevent other species from efficiently navigating fish ladders. Juvenile shad are thought to compete with native species of fish for food.

American shad, *Alosa sapidissima* (introduced)

Distinguishing Characteristics
Shad are laterally compressed and silvery in appearance. They have a saw-like, or serrated, "keel" along the belly, large cycloid scales, big eyes and a deeply forked tail.

Life History and Behavior
American shad reached the Columbia River in 1876 after being introduced into the Sacramento River, California, five years earlier. Shad are anadromous. They spend three to four years in the Pacific Ocean before returning to their natal stream as adults. They migrate upstream in the Columbia River as far as Priest Rapids Dam and to Lower Granite Dam on the Snake River.

One factor leading to increased shad populations in the Columbia River was inundation of Celilo Falls, a barrier to shad migration, by The Dalles Dam in 1957. A record 5.2 million adult shad were estimated to migrate up the Columbia River in 2005. At their peak, more than 350,000 shad per day passed Bonneville Dam, more than 200 fish every minute. The average size of shad in the Columbia River is 17 to 19 inches and 3 to 4 pounds. Females, often referred to as "roe shad," are typically larger than males.

Male American shad mature at 3 years of age and females a year later. Spawning occurs at water temperatures of 60 F to 65 F. The female swims near the surface and broadcasts tiny semibuoyant eggs in open water, primarily at night. Eggs drift downstream and settle in the substrate. Fry hatch in three to 10 days. Juvenile shad migrate downstream to the ocean in early fall when they are 3 inches to 4 inches long. They form dense, silvery schools that flash as they feed and move downstream.

American shad are primarily plankton feeders. Juvenile shad eat zooplankton and aquatic insect larvae. While in the ocean, shad use their long gill rakers to strain crustaceans and other small items from the water column.

Normally, adult shad do not feed during the upriver spawning migration. However, they readily strike small lures and flies and provide excellent sport on light tackle. Shad generally follow the Columbia and Snake river shorelines at depths of 8 feet to 25 feet. Dick Nite spoons in silver or red and white, fished near the bottom, are effective. Adult shad are good-eating if prepared properly. Their flesh should be baked slowly at low heat or pickled to soften the large number of bones. Sautéed roe and milt also are said to be savory table fare for the bold gourmet. Anglers interested in learning more about the history of American shad in the United States (as well as how to catch them) would do well by getting a copy of *The Founding Fish* by John McPhee.

Trout, Salmon, Chars and Whitefishes – Family Salmonidae

No other group of fishes generates as much excitement to the average sports angler as do salmon and trout where they are present. Indeed, Pacific Northwest residents are often referred to by those outside the region as "salmon-centric." Salmonids are coldwater fishes of the Northern Hemisphere. This family includes both anadromous and resident forms having a range of migratory behaviors.

All trout, salmon and char once shared a common gene pool with whitefish and grayling. Modern molecular biology, while showing that a common genetic origin exists among the many diverse species, has resulted in the present classification system. For example, rainbow and cutthroat trout were once included in the genus *Salmo* along with brown trout. Both species are now considered closer in origin to the five species of Pacific salmon within the genus *Oncorhynchus*.

As a group, salmonids are characterized by having small cycloid scales, an adipose fin and no spines or only soft rays in their fins. They all share the same basic streamlined shape, but many exhibit drastic changes during the breeding season, such as sexual dimorphism, that result in vivid color patterns or difference in the size and shape of the head.

Mountain whitefish, *Prosopium williamsoni* (native). Other common names include herring. A longer-nosed version of this species is sometimes referred to as chiselmouth jack or "Pinocchio."

Distinguishing Characteristics

Across North America, there are 20 different species of whitefish. Most live in northern latitudes where water temperatures tend to be cooler. Mountain whitefish have a small subterminal, slightly down-turned mouth, fewer than 100 scales along the lateral line and a single flap between the nostrils. Whitefish scales are much larger in size than salmon or trout scales, and their caudal fin is more deeply forked. They are sometimes mistaken for Arctic grayling. However, grayling have a larger mouth and a much longer dorsal fin (17 to 25 total rays) compared to whitefish. Whitefish also lack spots on the body.

Life History and Behavior

The mountain whitefish is the most abundant species of whitefish in Washington. Although stream populations are considered sedentary, some fish may move into tributary streams from the Columbia River to spawn. Columbia River tributaries with significant populations of mountain whitefish include the Umatilla, Walla Walla, Yakima, Wenatchee and Methow rivers. Mountain whitefish also migrate throughout the Columbia River, based on dam counts. Numbers increase markedly in the Hanford Reach when fish migrate upstream from the McNary Reservoir in the early fall.

Whitefish often form large schools of 100 fish or more before spawning. In smaller rivers, you might see them congregating in pools by looking when the sun shines into the water at the right angle.

Unlike salmon and trout, mountain whitefish do not build a nest. They broadcast eggs over gravel and cobble bottom and leave them to fend for themselves without parental care. Young mountain whitefish first appear along sandy shorelines in early March as tiny larvae. At this stage, they resemble a short rice noodle with goggle-like black eyes. They soon change into a more trout-like shape distinguishable from other small fishes by two horizontal rows of small black spots on their side. Young-of-the-year whitefish move offshore and migrate downstream about the time juvenile Chinook salmon emerge from redds.

Juvenile whitefish feed on aquatic insect larvae. Larger fish eat insect larvae, snails and plant material. They make a flash of silver as they turn to feed, using their pointed toothless mouth to deftly remove food items attached to the top and side of rocks. Larger whitefish may turn over small rocks with their rubbery nose when feeding.

Mountain whitefish provide good sport, readily striking small spinners, flies and bait. Winter anglers willing to brave icy conditions have good success drifting red- or orange-hackled flies tipped with maggots through riffles in the Yakima and Wenatchee rivers. Mountain whitefish stage near fall Chinook salmon spawning areas in the Hanford Reach in October and November to gorge on loose salmon eggs.

Mountain whitefish were cleverly sold as mountain herring in the 1870s to markets in Salt Lake City. They are tasty when smoked and, according to my mother, make a good fish soup. The state record for mountain whitefish, 5 pounds and 2 ounces, was caught at Vernita Bar, Columbia River in 1983.

Lake whitefish, *Coregonus clupeaformis* (introduced)

Distinguishing Characteristics

The two flaps between the nostrils of lake whitefish distinguish it from the mountain whitefish, which have a single flap. Additionally, larger specimens have a concave shape between the head and nape. Lake whitefish have a silvery-gray appearance but are deeper bodied and grow to a larger size than mountain whitefish.

Life History and Behavior

Lake whitefish were introduced into Lake Pend Oreille, Idaho, in 1889, where they moved downstream into the Columbia River system. They are now found from the U.S.-Canada border downstream to McNary Reservoir and are most abundant in Lake Roosevelt, Banks Lake and downstream to Chief Joseph reservoir. Lake whitefish prefer cold, deep lakes and tend to occupy pelagic, or open-water, habitats.

Lake whitefish mature at 4 to 5 years of age. Spawning occurs over gravel or sandy bottom, from October to January. Their eggs are semibuoyant and take approximately 30 days to hatch at 50 F. Young whitefish feed primarily on zooplankton. As they get larger, they shift their diet to bottom-dwelling, or benthic, invertebrates such as midge larvae. Adults are also bottom feeders but may occasionally eat small fish.

FISHES
Color Plates

Identify Columbia Basin fish visually with this color guide

p. 109
Pacific lamprey, *Lampetra tridentata* (26.5 inches)

p. 112
White sturgeon, *Acipenser transmontanus* (28 inches)

p. 115
American shad, *Alosa sapidissima* (female 22.5 inches)

p. 116
Mountain whitefish, *Prosopium williamsoni* (9.8 inches)

p. 118
Lake whitefish, *Coregonus clupeaformis* (16.5 inches)

p. 119
Bull trout, *Salvelinus confluentus* (22 inches)

p. 120
Brook trout, *Salvelinus fontinalis* (female, 8.3 inches)

p. 121
Lake trout, *Salvelinus namaycush* (18 inches)

p. 122
Cutthroat trout, *Oncorhynchus clarki*
(male intermountain form, 15.8 inches)

p. 123
Rainbow trout, *Oncorhynchus mykiss* (18.8 inches)

p. 123
Steelhead, *Oncorhynchus mykiss* (male, 29.5 inches)

p. 126
Brown trout, *Salmo trutta* (16.1 inches)

p. 126
Chinook or king salmon, *Oncorhynchus tshawytscha*
(male, 30 inches)

p. 126
Chinook or king salmon, *Oncorhynchus tshawytscha*
(female, 30 inches)

p. 129
Coho or silver salmon, *Oncorhynchus kisutch*
(male, 31.5 inches)

p. 129
Coho or silver salmon, *Oncorhynchus kisutch*
(female, 30.8 inches)

p. 130
Sockeye/kokanee or red salmon, *Oncorhynchus nerka*
(male, 27.2 inches)

p. 130
Sockeye/kokanee or red salmon, *Oncorhynchus nerka*
(female, 26.1 inches)

p. 132
Pink salmon or humpy, *Oncorhynchus gorbuscha*
(male, 27 inches)

p. 132
Pink salmon or humpy, *Oncorhynchus gorbuscha*
(female, 26.4 inches)

p. 133
Chum or dog salmon, *Oncorhynchus keta* (male, 33.2 inches)

p. 133
Chum or dog salmon, *Oncorhynchus keta* (female, 30.8 inches)

p. 134
Eulachon, *Thaleichthys pacificus* (7.7 inches)

p. 136
Grass pickerel, *Esox americanus* (8.9 inches)

p. 137
Common carp, *Cyprinus carpio* (19.8 inches)

p. 139
Tench, *Tinca tinca* (20.2 inches)

p. 140
Chiselmouth, *Acrocheilus alutaceus* (10.9 inches)

p. 140
Northern pikeminnow, *Ptychocheilus oregonensis* (20.1 inches)

p. 142
Redside shiner, *Richardsonius balteatus* (3.9 inches)

p. 142
Peamouth, *Mylocheiulus caurinus* (male, 9.3 inches)

p. 143
Longnose dace, *Rhinichthys cataractae* (4.9 inches)

p. 146
Largescale sucker, *Catostomus macrocheilus* (11.4 inches)

Bridgelip sucker, *Catostomus columbianus* (15.5 inches)

Mountain sucker, *Catostomus platyrhynchus* (3.5 inches)

Longnose sucker, *Catostomus catostomus* (17 inches)

Channel catfish, *Ictalurus punctatus* (10.5 inches)

p. 151
Brown bullhead, *Ameiurus nebulosus* (7.5 inches)

p. 153
Tadpole madtom, *Noturus gyrinus* (est. 3 inches)

p. 154
Banded killifish, *Fundulus diaphanus* (est. 3 inches)

p. 154
Western mosquitofish, *Gambusia affinis* (male, 1.1 inches)

p. 155
Burbot, *Lota lota* (29 inches)

p. 156
Three-spine stickleback, *Gasterosteus aculeatus* (2.5 inches)

p. 157
Sand roller, *Percopsis transmontana* (2.8 inches)

p. 158
Smallmouth bass, *Micropterus dolomieu* (12.7 inches)

p. 159
Largemouth bass, *Micropterus salmoides* (8 inches)

p. 161
Bluegill, *Lepomis macrochirus* (6 inches)

p. 162
Pumpkinseed, *Lepomis gibbosus* (4.2 inches)

p. 162
Black crappie, *Pomoxis nigromaculatus* (10.4 inches)

p. 164
Yellow perch, *Perca flavescens* (10.8 inches)

p. 165
Walleye, *Sander vitreus* (16.7 inches)

p. 167
Prickly sculpin, *Cottus asper* (4.3 inches)

p. 168
Torrent sculpin, *Cottus rhotheus* (2.5 inches)

Author Dennis Dauble on the Columbia River

Fishes
of the
COLUMBIA BASIN

Lake whitefish were once fished commercially in the United States and Canada. They are not a popular sport fish but may be taken by fishing on the bottom with bait or jigs. Their white flesh is tasty, especially when smoked. The state angling record of 27 inches and 6 pounds, 10 ounces was taken from Lake Roosevelt in 1997.

Bull trout, *Salvelinus confluentus* (native)

For many years, the names Dolly Varden and bull trout were synonymous with a single species. Bull trout, considered an inland species of char, were first described as a separate species in 1978. The anadromous or migratory form, Dolly Varden, is limited to waters north of Puget Sound. Dolly Varden were named after a popular color and pattern of polka dots used in dressmaking. Dolly Varden and bull trout are so similar in appearance that genetic analysis might be required to differentiate between them where ranges overlap.

Distinguishing Characteristics
Bull trout tend to have a robust and flattened head. Their body is covered with cream to crimson spots on an olive-green background. They have very small scales, typically 190 to 240 along the lateral line. The dorsal fin has no spots and the anal fin has a white margin.

Life History and Behavior
Bull trout are mainly restricted to cool headwater streams and are rarely found in the main stem Columbia and Snake rivers. They remain widely distributed across their potential range, although many areas support only remnant populations. Because of patchy distribution, habitat fragmentation from migration barriers or habitat degradation has affected migratory patterns and restricted movement. Bull trout are common in headwaters of the Grande Ronde, Yakima, Walla Walla, Tucannon and John Day river systems. A small population also exists in the Lake Pend Oreille system, migrating seasonally between lake and riverine habitats. In some areas, their numbers are limited by habitat quality, interactions with non-native species and lack of a migratory life history.

Adult bull trout favor deep pools in streams, particularly where woody debris and log jams are present. Young-of-year generally seek side channels and shallow, nearshore areas of low velocity. Bull trout may have limited migrations relating to spawning and rearing. For example, after they spawn, subadults and adults may move downstream to larger streams or reservoir/lake habitats.

Bull trout spawn in early fall as water temperatures decline to less than 48 F. Hatching occurs in about 200 days. Newly hatched alevins, or fry, average 1 inch long. The diet of juvenile bull trout is primarily aquatic insect larvae. Their diet shifts to fish as they get larger.

In eastern Washington streams, bull trout may reach 8 inches in length by age 3. They mature at age 5 to 6 and grow to a large size where not exploited by anglers. Hybridization is common where bull trout and brook trout occur together.

Bull trout are relatively easy to catch; thus, they are subject to overharvest by anglers. Although their pink flesh has excellent flavor, don't eat one. Columbia Basin populations have been listed as threatened under the Endangered Species Act since 1998. Overall, bull trout are in need of effective conservation management. The Washington State angling record was a 35-inch, 22.5-pound fish taken from the Tieton River (Yakima River drainage) in 1961. The Oregon record is a 23-pound, 2-ounce specimen taken from Lake Billy Chinook (upper Deschutes River drainage).

Brook trout, *Salvelinus fontinalis* (introduced). Other common names include speckled trout, aurora trout, brookie, square-tail, mud trout and mountain trout. Brook trout have been crossed with brown trout to create so-called "tiger trout" and with lake trout to create "splake."

Distinguishing Characteristics

Brook trout are the only trout having vermiculations, or wavelike markings, on the back and dorsal fins. The leading edges of the anal and pelvic fins have black and white borders. "Brookies" are olive-green to dark brown on their back and have small crimson spots surrounded by blue halos on their sides. The sides and belly of males intensify and become orange-red at spawning. Their tail is more squared off than lake trout and they have fewer pyloric caeca (range 25 to 50).

Life History and Behavior

Brook trout are endemic to the northeastern part of the United States and were introduced widely because of their appeal as a sport fish. They are common in some high mountain lakes or beaver ponds where they have been stocked but are rare in Columbia Basin streams. Brook trout are considered a threat to native populations of rainbow trout where they are abundant. They also cross with native bull trout populations where distribution overlaps.

Brook trout spawn in tributaries to lakes or along shorelines in gravelly areas where groundwater upwelling occurs. They spawn in the fall, and eggs hatch four to five months later. Young fish feed on zooplankton and aquatic insect larvae. The diet of larger fish also includes terrestrial insects and fish such as sculpin.

Brook trout grow slowly and often become overpopulated and stunted in high mountain lakes, although they may attain larger sizes in some waters. A 5-year-old brook trout may be only 6 to 8 inches long in Washington streams.

Brook trout are the favorite of many anglers. They readily take bait, flies and small spinners. Brook trout are stocked in many higher-elevation lakes. The Washington state record of 24.5 inches and 9 pounds was taken from Wobbly Lake in 1988. The Oregon record of 9 pounds, 6 ounces was from the Deschutes River in 1980.

Lake trout, *Salvelinus namaycush* (introduced). Other common names include laker, gray trout, mackinaw and lake char. Lake trout crossed with brook trout in hatcheries produce hybrids known as "splake" or "wendigo."

Distinguishing Characteristics
The caudal fin is deeply forked. Their sides are typically gray with many white or pale-yellow spots, but no red spots. They have 90 to 200 pyloric caeca and white borders on lower fins.

Life History and Behavior
Lake trout are the largest species of char. They are restricted to freshwater and cannot tolerate high salinity. Lake trout have limited distribution in the Columbia Basin. They were widely introduced in eastern Washington to Loon Lake and Deer Lake, among others. They prefer cold, deep water and reside near the bottom. Lake trout are solitary and do not school except during spawning.

Lake trout mature at 6 to 7 years when they are 14 to 19 inches long. They spawn in the fall in gravel-rubble shoals of lakes where wave action keeps the substrate clean. They do not build a redd or defend territories. Young lake trout eat crustaceans and insects. Larger trout shift to mainly a fish diet.

Lake trout are sought after by anglers because of their large size. Their flesh is firm and has a good flavor. A popular method includes trolling weighted lines near the bottom with large, wobbling spoons. The Washington state record of 33 pounds, 7 ounces was taken from Lake Chelan in 2001.

Cutthroat trout, *Oncorhynchus clarki* (native). Other common names include Clark's trout, red-throated trout and sea trout.

Distinguishing Characteristics

There are several subspecies of cutthroat trout in the Pacific Northwest, each with slight differences in appearance. When compared to rainbow trout, their maxillary, or upper jawbone, is long, extending beyond the posterior margin of the eye. In addition, cutthroat trout have basibranchial, or hyoid teeth, behind the tongue and between the second gill cleft. The cutthroat trout usually has red-orange slash marks on the underside of the lower jaw and 150 to 180 scales in the lateral line.

Life History and Behavior

The first-known description of cutthroat trout in western North America was Lewis and Clark's "speckled or mountain trout," documented in 1805 near the headwaters of the Missouri River. According to noted trout biologist Robert Behnke, the original distribution of cutthroat trout is greater than for any other salmonid species in North America except for lake trout. Unlike rainbow trout, cutthroat trout have rarely become established outside their native range.

The primary subspecies native to the Mid-Columbia region is the westslope cutthroat trout. Its historical distribution was in Lake Chelan, Methow River basin and the headwaters of the Pend Oreille River. Hatchery-reared fish from Stehekin on Lake Chelan were stocked in alpine lakes and streams throughout Washington in the early 20th century. Subsequently, populations of westslope cutthroat spread throughout the lower Snake River and tributaries of the upper Columbia River. Cutthroat trout are rare in the main stem Columbia River upstream of Bonneville Dam. They have been displaced in some streams by rainbow and brook trout.

The coastal form predominates downstream of Bonneville Dam. Cutthroat trout are considered anadromous in some tributaries of the lower Columbia River and may spend most of their life in the estuary. Coastal cutthroats are generally declining throughout their range. Depressed stocks in the lower Columbia River are supplemented by hatchery releases.

In general, cutthroat trout are sensitive to changes in water quality, especially increases in water temperature. One subspecies, the Lahontan, has been stocked in inland lakes such as Omak and Lenore because of its tolerance for high levels of alkalinity and salinity.

Westslope cutthroat trout spawn in spring and early summer on an ascending temperature cycle. Similar to other salmonids, they dig a redd in river gravels. Newly emerged cutthroat feed on zooplankton and other microscopic animal life. They shift their diet to aquatic insect larvae and terrestrial insects as they grow. Larger cutthroat trout may prey on small fishes such as minnows.

Cutthroat trout exhibit slow growth rates and may attain 6 inches to 10 inches in length by age 6 in Washington streams. Adfluvial and fluvial populations that spend more time in lakes or larger streams typically attain larger sizes.

The primary recreational opportunities for westslope cutthroat trout occur on the east slope of the Cascade Mountains above 3,000 feet in elevation and in selected northeastern Washington streams. The John Day River of central Oregon also contains westslope cutthroat trout.

Cutthroat trout are considered to be the easiest of all trout to catch. Mid-Columbia fisheries, such as Lenore Lake, attract hordes of fly fishers during the spring spawning interval.

Rainbow trout and steelhead, *Oncorhynchus mykiss* (native). Other common names include Kamloops trout. Beginning with the original designation of a rainbow trout *Salmo gairdnerii* from the Columbia River in 1836, rainbow trout have been tagged with 25 different scientific names! This is no surprise given all the variation in color, scale number and other features. However, modern genetic analysis has since proven that all subspecies, including the mythical golden trout that I once hiked 15 miles for but came up empty, should be included within the full species *O. mykiss*.

Distinguishing Characteristics
The resident form of rainbow trout have larger scales than cutthroat trout (fewer than 150 along the lateral line) and usually lack an orange throat slash. Spotting patterns and coloration are generally too variable between the two species to consistently distinguish.

The anadromous form, steelhead, is generally narrower bodied than salmon, and the back of their caudal fin is more square. They also have a smaller mouth. The maxillary, or upper jawbone, does not extend beyond the eye. Another key feature is that steelhead have 10 to 12 anal fin rays compared to Chinook and coho salmon, which have 14 to 19 and 13 to 16 rays, respectively.

Life History and Behavior

The rainbow trout is the best-known species of trout in the world. There are considered to be two major forms of rainbow trout: the resident rainbow and the sea-going, or anadromous, steelhead. Robert Behnke further categorizes each type into subspecies native to the Columbia and Northern Great basins. Current nomenclature in the Columbia Basin includes Kamloops-type rainbow trout from Lake Pend Oreille and the famous Deschutes River "redside," a unique subspecies also called "desert red band trout."

Many Northwest river systems contain both rainbow trout and steelhead. Genetic background determines the tendency of rainbow trout to migrate to the ocean or stay in their home stream. Environmental conditions such as high water temperature, high population density or low flow also may trigger downstream movement of juvenile rainbow trout. Resident trout may complete their entire life cycle within a 100-foot section of stream, while steelhead migrate hundreds of miles to the Pacific Ocean and back.

The native range of steelhead is the eastern Pacific Ocean and freshwater west of the Rocky Mountains from Baja, Mexico, to Alaska, and the Kamchatka Peninsula. Over the past 50 years or so, this popular fish has been transplanted to all parts of the world including New Zealand and Chile. I once fished in the Great Lakes for a "Skamania" strain of steelhead imported from Washington.

Adult steelhead migrate upstream in the Columbia River during most months of the year with peak runs occurring during the late summer. Some steelhead swim upstream at the rate of 30 to 40 miles per day, while others dip into cool-water tributaries when main stem water temperatures are high. Steelhead from the Columbia Basin include Snake River populations commonly referred to as "A-run" or "B-run." The difference has to do with run timing over Bonneville Dam and size at maturity. The A-run migrates earlier, passing upstream of Bonneville Dam in June to August, and are predominantly one-ocean fish (spend one year in the ocean before returning to freshwater to spawn). They average 4 pounds to 6 pounds in size. The B-run generally passes in August to October. They typically spend two years in the ocean and average 8 pounds to 12 pounds, or larger.

Migrating adult steelhead ascend spawning streams in the Columbia Basin from September through February. They often stage in main stem reservoirs until fall rains replenish the parched basin, moving upriver with successive rain and snowmelt events until they reach spawning grounds. Unlike salmon, which spawn in the fall, steelhead hold over and spawn the following spring. They construct redds in gravel bottom areas of moderate velocity. Steelhead are unique for the genus *Oncorhynchus* in that a portion of those who survive spawning have a post-spawning adult, or kelt, stage that migrates downstream to the Pacific Ocean before returning to spawn again in a different year.

Steelhead eggs incubate in the gravel for two to three months before they hatch. After the juveniles emerge from their gravel nests, they rear in tributary streams for usually two years until they become "smolts" and migrate to the Pacific Ocean. Juvenile steelhead that remain in freshwater their entire life are considered rainbow trout.

In the Hanford Reach of the Columbia River, juvenile steelhead migrate in the deepest part of the river, the "thalwag," and near the bottom. Most migration occurs at night. Daytime behavior includes resting and feeding near shore. In contrast, juvenile steelhead in reservoirs of the Columbia and Snake rivers tend to be more surface-oriented. This behavior makes them vulnerable to fish-eating birds, such as the Caspian tern.

The resident form of rainbow trout also spawn in the spring. Although they may overlap in distribution with steelhead, trout normally select smaller substrate. Growth rates of stream resident rainbow trout are highly variable depending on water temperature and food supply. Fry feed on zooplankton and insect larvae. Terrestrial insects comprise a large percentage of the diet of larger fish in the summer.

Most Columbia Basin waterways have an 8-inch size limit for rainbow trout. Opening day in area streams is delayed until late spring to ensure that juvenile steelhead or smolt migrate safely downstream and are not harvested. Stocking of hatchery steelhead smolt and rainbow trout is a concern where they might displace resident populations. Standard management practices of put-and-take rainbow trout fisheries focus on lakes and ponds for greatest benefit to anglers.

Rainbow trout and steelhead are known for tremendous fighting ability that includes acrobatic leaps and long runs. They will take bait, spinners, spoons or rise to the fly. Both rainbow trout and steelhead are excellent table fare with flesh ranging from bright orange to white depending on their diet and condition. The

Snake River record steelhead was a 48.5-inch-long, 35-pound, 1-ounce fish taken in 1973. A 25-plus pound rainbow trout taken from Rufus Woods Lake in the upper Columbia in 1998 was from the local triploid fishery.

Brown trout, *Salmo trutta* (introduced). Other common names include German brown and brownie. Brown trout have been crossed with brook trout to create so-called "tiger trout."

Distinguishing Characteristics

Brown trout are light brown on the back and differ from other trouts in having dark spots on the sides of the body that are surrounded by halos. They may have irregular-shaped red spots on their sides. Juvenile brown trout have an orange adipose fin.

Life History and Behavior

Brown trout were introduced to the eastern United States from Europe in 1883. Subsequently, they were stocked in many streams and lakes of Washington State in the early 20th century. Brown trout are considered to be more tolerant of poor water quality conditions than other species of trout. They are secretive and feed primarily at night or dawn and dusk. Brown trout have a greater rod-to-cone cell ratio in the retina of their eye compared to rainbow, cutthroat and brook trout. This characteristic is thought to improve vision under conditions of low light.

Brown trout spawn in the late fall. Both male and female trout defend their redd. Eggs hatch in the spring after developing in the gravel for approximately 50 days. Newly emerged fry feed on small aquatic insects. Larger trout are carnivorous. They eat crayfish, aquatic insects and small fish. Brown trout grow fast and may reach 12 inches in length by age 3.

Although brown trout grow to a large size, they are considered to be the most difficult of all trout to catch. Local populations of brown trout are in the Tucannon and Touchet rivers in southeastern Washington, along with several inland lakes. The Washington state record of 36 inches, 22 pounds was taken in 1963 in Sullivan Lake.

Chinook salmon, *Oncorhynchus tshawytscha* (native). Other common names include king salmon, tyee salmon, spring salmon and quinnat salmon.

Distinguishing Characteristics

Chinook salmon are the largest of all Pacific salmon. They have large spots on both lobes of the caudal fin and black gums around the teeth of the lower jaw. Their tail is slightly forked as compared to the more square tail of a steelhead. Anal fin rays range from 14 to 19. They also have the largest number of pyloric caeca (more than 100) of all salmon and steelhead. Chinook fry and smolt are distinguished by having large parr marks that are bisected by the lateral line.

Life History and Behavior

The natural range of Chinook salmon extends from northern Alaska to the Ventura River in Southern California. The center of abundance is the Columbia River system where historical run size was as high as 10 million fish per year. Current abundance is on the order of 2 million adults and is largely composed of hatchery fish.

Spring-run Chinook salmon, or "springers," have a stream-type life history in the Columbia River, i.e., they spend one to two years in freshwater before migrating to the Pacific Ocean. As returning adults, they are first to enter the estuary, and most pass upriver to tributary streams by mid-June. In contrast, both summer- and fall-run, or ocean-type, Chinook salmon rear for two to four months in their natal stream before migrating downstream. Most summer Chinook salmon return to spawning grounds or hatcheries in large tributaries of the upper Columbia River.

The principal run of fall Chinook salmon, the "upriver bright" population, spawns in the Hanford Reach of the mid-Columbia region. This population is distinguished by the time of year they enter the river, their silvery skin color and orange flesh having a high oil content. A second population of Columbia River fall Chinook salmon, the "tule," has a darker appearance and lighter-colored flesh when they enter the lower river. These characteristics make them less valuable for sport and commercial catch.

Female Chinook salmon select a suitable spawning site, usually near a sloping gravel bar in water depths typically 6 to 12 feet deep. One or more males soon join her and she deposits up to 5,000 eggs in a gravel-cobble nest (redd) dug with her tail. After spawning, salmon defend their territory for a week or two, then hang out in nearshore areas until they die. Fishes that die after they spawn once are termed semelparous. Spawned-out salmon become easy prey for predators such as bald eagles that return to the Hanford Reach each year to spend the winter. Dead salmon stack like cordwood in deep pools of rivers. Their carcasses drift slowly downstream and decompose; associated nutrients become part of the aquatic food chain.

Juvenile salmon emerge from their gravel nests in early spring. Small animals such as midge larvae and zooplankton are important in their diet early on. As juvenile salmon grow and move from the shallows to deeper water, their diet switches to caddisfly adult and terrestrial insects. Juvenile fall, or ocean-type, Chinook salmon begin to migrate downstream during June and July of their first year. Their migration behavior is less directed than yearling smolts. Some subyearling salmon may not reach the Columbia River estuary until late summer or early fall. Spring, or stream-type, Chinook salmon migrate downstream as yearlings. These larger smolts are surface-oriented in main stem reservoirs of the Snake and Columbia rivers but may migrate at deeper depths in the Hanford Reach.

Most juvenile, ocean-type Chinook salmon disperse north along the Pacific Coast to British Columbia and southern Alaska. In contrast, stream-type Chinook salmon migrate both north and south of the Columbia River mouth, as far north as the Bering Sea, and farther offshore. These differences make for interesting issues between commercial fishermen from the United States and Canada who harvest salmon from international waters.

When adult Chinook salmon return to freshwater two to five years later, they migrate to the exact stream from which they hatched, a behavior known as homing. Scientists believe this ability is due to powerful olfactory senses. One theory proposes that salmon imprint, or become sensitized to some odor, perhaps to a metal or combination of organic substances present in the water during their early rearing period. This memory helps guide them when they swim back to their natal area or place of birth.

Chinook salmon are the least abundant of the five species of North American Pacific salmon, accounting for about 5 percent of the total commercial catch. They are, however, one of the most popular sport fishing species in the Mid-Columbia region. Madness begins when adult spring Chinook salmon return to the lower Columbia River in April and May and doesn't end until the fall run begins to spawn in mid-October.

Salmon fishing is often best off the mouth of larger tributaries where fish pause and also in the vicinity of spawning grounds. Although bank fishing is an option, most Chinook salmon are caught from boats. Anglers troll near the bottom with a wide variety of gear, including Magnum WiggleWarts, Kwikfish wrapped with sardine meat, flashers with herring and large spinners. Drift fishing or back-trolling roe is also effective. It may take many hours on the water to catch a salmon, but the reward can be great. There are few culinary delights better than a freshly caught salmon grilled over the coals.

Coho salmon, *Oncorhynchus kisutch* (native). Other common names include silver salmon.

Distinguishing Characteristics

Adult coho salmon have spots only on the upper lobe of the caudal fin and white gums on the lower jaw. Juvenile coho salmon have an elongated anal fin ray. Their parr marks are bisected by the lateral line and narrower than the interspaces.

Life History and Behavior

Coho salmon were once abundant in tributaries of the upper Columbia and Snake rivers, including the Yakima and Methow rivers. However, several factors contributed to their decline, including overharvest, logging practices, construction of dams for irrigation and hydroelectric power, reduction of off-channel rearing habitat, and de-watering of tributary streams. Consequently, natural migrations to the Columbia Basin largely disappeared by the mid-1970s. Current populations of coho salmon are supplemented by hatcheries. Several efforts are under way by tribal and state fisheries managers to reestablish runs. In the Mid-Columbia region, coho runs are restricted to the Methow, Wenatchee, Yakima, Umatilla and Klickitat rivers.

Adult coho migrate upstream in the late summer and fall. In male coho, the upper jaw forms an elongated, hooked snout and teeth become greatly enlarged. The lower jaw also elongates and may become knobbed. Females construct redds in gravel beds of small streams and spawn, usually from November through January. After spawning, the adult dies.

Eggs incubate in the river over the winter and fry hatch in six to eight weeks depending on water temperature. They emerge from redds approximately two weeks after hatching, then remain in freshwater for one to two years before becoming smolts. Smolts migrate to the ocean in April to May at 3 inches to 6 inches in length. Stream-dwelling coho consume mainly insects but also may prey on other fish. In Columbia River reservoirs, juvenile coho feed on zooplankton and aquatic insects.

Coho salmon are a wonderful sport fish. They are good eating and much prized by anglers. Much of the recreational fishery on the Oregon and Washington coast is geared toward coho salmon. Similar to other Pacific salmon, coho don't feed once they begin migrating upstream in the Columbia River. However, they aggressively take bait, spinners, flies and jigs. An early historical record from the Mid-Columbia region was by John Gantenheim of Pasco, who reportedly caught a "silverside" from the Columbia River near the mouth of the Yakima River while trolling a spoon August 20, 1893.

From 1962 to 1979, runs to the Snake River made up one-third of the upriver Columbia Basin run, averaging 3,800 fish in 1968. Former returns were likely at the limits of their migration range. Coho salmon are now extinct in the Snake River. Within the Columbia Basin, the Klickitat, Umatilla and Yakima rivers support runs of hatchery coho salmon with limited harvest opportunity for sport anglers.

Sockeye salmon, *Oncorhynchus nerka* (native). Other common names include red salmon and blueback salmon. The landlocked form, or kokanee, is often called little redfish and silver trout.

Distinguishing Characteristics
Adult sockeye salmon lack distinct dark spots on their backs and caudal fin. They exhibit a green head and red body at spawning. Sockeye salmon also have 28 to 40 long, slender gill rakers on the first gill arch. This characteristic distinguishes them from all other Pacific salmon, which have fewer, stout gill rakers. Juvenile sockeye salmon are more slender in appearance than coho or Chinook salmon. Their parr marks are small, oval in shape and centered above the lateral line.

Life History and Behavior
Sockeye salmon are the second most-abundant species of Pacific salmon, accounting for 25 percent of the commercial catch. Sockeye salmon in the Columbia River are the southernmost major run in North America. The largest runs occur in Canada and Alaska. Sockeye salmon differ from other species of Pacific salmon in requiring a lake for part of their life cycle. Adults dig redds and spawn in the gravel of inlet or outlet streams. They die soon after spawning. Eggs incubate in the gravel over the winter, and fry hatch in the spring. Soon after they emerge fry migrate to a lake where they rear for one to two years before migrating to the ocean. Juvenile sockeye salmon feed on zooplankton in freshwater.

Sockeye salmon feed on large crustaceans at sea for two to four years before they mature and return to natal areas. The adult migration interval in the Columbia River occurs in midsummer with peak movement over lower Columbia River dams in July. Spawning is earlier than for Chinook and coho salmon, occurring from mid-September to late October. Adult sockeye salmon are smaller than Chinook and coho salmon. They typically range from 4 pounds to 8 pounds. Breeding males develop a compressed body, hooked snout and a small hump before the dorsal fin.

Important production areas for sockeye salmon in the Columbia River include Lake Osoyoos and Lake Wenatchee in the Okanogan and Wenatchee river systems, respectively. Historically, the run size of sockeye salmon from the Snake River was estimated at 150,000 fish. However, sockeye salmon declined toward extinction soon after the impassable Hells Canyon complex was completed in the late 1960s. Runs have averaged less than 100 fish per year since 1981. Population rebuilding measures, including a captive brood stock program, have been in effect after Redfish Lake sockeye salmon populations were listed in 1991 for protection under the Endangered Species Act. A famous member of the brood stock program was nicknamed "Lonesome Larry" after being the sole-surviving male to return to the Snake River. His sperm was cryopreserved so that future generations might populate these waters. Native populations in the Snake River remain, for all practical purposes, extinct.

Kokanee, or the freshwater resident form of sockeye salmon, are derived from anadromous runs. Kokanee were established in the upper Columbia and Snake River basins before access to the ocean was blocked by hydroelectric dams. Sockeye salmon and kokanee were thought to be a separate species when first described by U.S. Army surgeon George Suckley in 1862. When the two forms were first observed in the late 19th century, naturalists called them "big redfish" and "little redfish," respectively. The sockeye morphology has since been observed in rivers where they are now thought extinct. Some biologists attribute Snake River returns to outmigrating kokanee that escaped downstream over impassable hydroelectric projects.

Natural spawning populations of kokanee occur in Lake Coeur d'Alene and Lake Roosevelt in the upper Columbia River, Lake Billy Chinook in the Deschutes River, and Wallowa Lake in the Grande Ronde systems. Populations that rear in reservoirs behind dams spawn in inlet streams or along the lakeshore. The sight of their small, scarlet bodies packed into tributaries to spawn in late summer is one to behold.

Adult sockeye salmon are rarely taken by sport fishermen in the Columbia Basin except in Lake Wenatchee, or Lake "Brewster," in years of special harvest. Plain red hooks trolled behind a flasher is a common angling technique. Those serious about catching adult sockeye salmon travel north to the Kenai River in Alaska where combat fishing is practiced or to Lake Washington near Seattle. Sockeye have red flesh when in their prime and are the most delicious of all Pacific salmon.

Landlocked sockeye salmon, or kokanee, provide significant sport-fishing opportunity in high mountain lakes on the east slope of the Cascades within the Yakima River drainage and in reservoirs of northeastern Washington state, including Lake Chelan, Lake Roosevelt and Loon Lake. These fish average 8 inches to 15 inches in length and provide excellent table fare. Kokanee generally prefer water temperatures near 50 F and congregate at lower depths when lakes stratify in the summer. Kokanee are caught by still-fishing with bait, by trolling and fly fishing. Trolling rigs usually consist of a flasher such as a "Ford Fender" followed by a series of beads and a baited hook. Kokanee fight hard but have a soft mouth that often leads to lost fish and disappointed anglers.

Pink salmon, *Oncorhynchus gorbuscha* (native). Other common names include humpback or humpy.

Distinguishing Characteristics

Pink salmon have large, oblong spots on the back and both lobes of the caudal fin; they are fine scaled with more than 169 scales on the lateral line. They are steel blue and silver in the ocean. Breeding males are reddish brown on their sides with olive-green blotches.

Life History and Behavior

Pink salmon are the most abundant and smallest of all Pacific salmon. They are rarely encountered upstream of Bonneville Dam in the Columbia River system. Pink salmon generally spawn from August to October usually within a short distance of the mouth of rivers. Fry move downstream immediately after emergence in the early winter and spring.

Pink salmon undergo a major change in body form as they approach sexual maturity. The male develops an enormous hump on the back and a greatly enlarged head. Their teeth enlarge on both the upper and lower jaws to form a pronounced, hooked kype. Some become compressed laterally. Females experience only minor changes in body shape. The average size of an adult is 20 inches and 4 pounds. They have a two-year life cycle, spending more than a year in the ocean, that generally coincides with odd-numbered calendar years.

Pink salmon are rarely harvested in the lower Columbia River sport fishery. However, they will aggressively strike small lures and flies early in the spawning run. The low fat content of their flesh makes them less desirable when compared to Chinook, coho and sockeye salmon.

Chum salmon, *Oncorhynchus keta* (native). Other common names include dog or calico salmon.

Distinguishing Characteristics
Chum salmon lack black spots on the back and tail fin. They have 19 to 20 short, thick gill rakers.

Life History and Behavior
Chum salmon are second only to Chinook salmon in body size. They are found in the Columbia Basin upstream to the Wind River. Small populations also occur in the Sandy River and downstream of Bonneville Dam. The population status of chum salmon was sufficiently precarious in the Columbia River that they were listed as threatened under the Endangered Species Act in 1999.

The average size of an adult is 28 inches and 10 to 12 pounds. Soon after entering freshwater, chum salmon develop greenish or dusky mottling on the sides. Mature males have reddish-purple vertical markings, and teeth of the lower jaw elongate. Chum salmon are not leapers. They are reluctant to enter long-span fish ladders or pass other migration barriers of significance in a river.

Like pink salmon, chum salmon have a lack of dependence on freshwater for feeding and growth. Fry migrate downstream quickly after their emergence in the spring and spend two to six months in the estuary. Chum stay in saltwater for three to five years before returning to spawn in October and November.

Few chum salmon are taken in the Columbia River sport fishery, although they will strike flies and lures, being partial to the color red. The skin of mature adults thickens during the spawning migration sufficiently enough that it has been marketed as "salmon leather." The flesh is cream-colored to pale pink and lowest of all salmons in fat content. Their common name "dog" is due to their being used as food for sled dogs in the north. Ocean-caught fish of higher quality are sometimes sold as "silver bryte" salmon.

Smelts – Family Osmeridae

There is only one member of this family in the Columbia Basin.

Eulachon, *Thaleichthys pacificus* (native). Other common names include Columbia River smelt, hooligan, candlefish, salvation fish and fathom fish.

Distinguishing Characteristics
Eulachon resemble a small trout or whitefish except they have a long anal fin (18 to 23 rays) and lack spots. They have small, pointed teeth on the jaws and in the mouth. Adults are brown to blue-black on top of their head and back, and their sides are silvery white. Ripe males have tubercles on their head.

Life History and Behavior
Eulachon is an anadromous smelt that moves short distances up the lower Columbia River and tributaries downstream of Bonneville Dam to spawn. They first enter the Columbia River in December and January with peak spawning migration in February and March. Males are the first to migrate. Females broadcast thousands of adhesive eggs that hatch in two to three weeks at 40 F to 46 F. Larvae are carried by water currents downstream to the estuary. Eulachon are important forage fish for other fishes, fish-eating birds and marine mammals.

Eulachon feed primarily on small crustaceans. Females mature at 3 to 4 years of age and 4 to 6 inches in length. Eulachon may reach a maximum size of 8 inches.

The flesh of eulachon is soft and sweet when cooked. There is a substantial sport fishery for eulachon. They are typically harvested by long-handled dip nets. The Cowlitz, Lewis and Sandy rivers have the largest runs, although numbers are declining.

Pikes – Family Esocidae

There are two members of this family in the Columbia Basin.

Northern pike, *Esox lucius* (introduced). Other common names may include pickerel or jackfish.

Distinguishing Characteristics

The opercle, or gill, cover has no scales. They have five sensory pores on each side of the lower jaw and 14 to 16 branchiostegals. The dorsal surface, upper sides and top of the head are brilliant green to olive brown.

Life History and Behavior

Introduction of northern pikes may turn out to be a bad idea, particularly if they expand their range into the Columbia River. There's a good reason that David Starr Jordan, a famous ichthyologist, called them "mere machines for the assimilation of other organisms." They are fierce predators and one of the fastest growing of all freshwater fishes.

Northern pikes are currently restricted to the Spokane River drainage in northeastern Washington. They generally prefer vegetative cover in slow-moving water; hence, they thrive in lakes, reservoirs and large rivers where there is abundant prey. They feed by sight during daylight hours. Northern pike tend to lie motionless until forage fish are within easy striking distance. Adults are believed to be capable of swimming 8 mph to 10 mph. They start eating other fishes when they are only 2 inches long.

Northern pikes may grow to 4 feet long and live more than 20 years. Males mature at 13 inches to 17 inches and 2 years to 5 years. Females mature when they reach 16 inches to 19 inches and 3 years to 6 years. Eggs are broadcast over submerged vegetation in the spring at water temperatures greater than 47 F.

Northern pikes are readily caught with live bait where legal. Elsewhere, large spoons, plugs and bucktail spinners are effective. They are speared through the ice in Minnesota. Two issues with catching and keeping northern pikes include needle-sharp teeth and the fact that they slime up when landed. Northern pikes are not a favorite culinary object for local anglers due to abundant "y," or intramuscular bones, that need to be removed before cooking and eating. The Washington state record is 44 inches at 32 pounds, 3 ounces caught from Long Lake in Spokane County.

Grass pickerel, *Esox americanus* (introduced)

Distinguishing Characteristics

The opercle or gill cover is completely scaled. They have four sensory pores on each side of the lower jaw and 11 to 12 branchiostegals.

Life History and Behavior

Grass pickerels are found in the Little Spokane River and several lakes, including Downs, Sprague, Horseshoe and Long lakes. They also were planted in the Palouse River drainage. This occurrence likely led to recent observations of grass pickerel in the Tucannon River, a tributary of the Snake River.

Grass pickerels have similar habitat preferences as northern pikes. They frequent lakes, ponds and backwaters of streams and rivers. They are extremely hardy and can tolerate water temperatures up to 84 F.

Grass pickerels spawn in the spring and summer by broadcasting their eggs on vegetation. Young pickerels eat insect larvae and crustaceans. Larger pickerels eat other fish. They may only reach a maximum length of 10 inches in Washington. Grass pickerels are not widely sought by anglers due to their small size and abundance of intramuscular bones.

Minnows – Family Cyprinidae

Minnows are distinguished from most other stream fishes by virtue of their fins being soft-rayed. That said, the leading edge of the dorsal and anal fins of carp and goldfish has a strong, serrated spine. Minnows can be brown, gold or silver, and some have stripes. Size has nothing to do with their classification. Minnows have a mouth that usually points forward and a thin, smooth lower lip without the little wart-like nubs that suckers have.

Minnows are not generally sought by local fishermen, but they provide occasional sport when hooked on light tackle. During extensive fisheries surveys of Hanford Reach fishes during the 1970s and 1980s, minnows were the most abundant group, comprising more than half of the total fish population by number. However, the local list of a dozen or so minnows is low in comparison with rivers in the eastern United States where up to 50 minnow species may be encountered.

Minnows start spawning in midsummer when water warms up to swimming temperatures. The eggs are broadcast in shallow water, hatch into fry that hide near submerged plants until they are large enough to venture offshore. Although minnows are considered resident fishes, individuals migrate great distances throughout the main stem Columbia River and tributaries to spawn or when searching for food.

Several species of minnows have special club cells in their skin that secrete an alarm substance if the skin is damaged. The release of this substance causes an immediate change in the schooling behavior of their peers.

The English author Izaak Walton, in his classic discourse on fishing *The Compleat Angler*, devoted several chapters describing how to catch and eat obscure members of the minnow family. According to Walton, a properly prepared chub is "a much better dish of meat than you ... do imagine." While the meat of most minnows has a palatable flavor, their rib bones have a "y" shape that makes it difficult to get a mouthful down. Scoring the ribs and cooking the fillets for a long time at low heat is one way to try native minnow fare.

Carp, *Cyprinus carpio* (introduced)

Common carp were introduced to the United States from Asia in the mid-19th century and quickly spread westward advertised as "the greatest food fish ever." Although most management efforts are now directed at eradicating carp where they compete with game fish and waterfowl, they have market value as both human and fish food.

"Mirror" carp are a form of the common carp. Mirror carp are distinguished by having only a few very large scales on the sides of the body. Koi are an ornamental form of common carp found in private fish ponds.

Distinguishing Characteristics
Common carp have a spine in both dorsal and anal fins and two distinct barbels on each side of the upper jaw. They have large scales on their body that umbricate or overlap, similar to shingles on a roof.

Life History and Behavior
Common carp are found throughout the Columbia and Snake rivers and lower reaches of large tributaries. They also occur in numerous lakes and ponds of the greater Columbia Basin. Carp inhabit shallow nearshore areas usually near vegeta-

tion. They are tolerant of adverse water quality conditions such as low dissolved oxygen, high water temperature, turbidity and pollutants.

Carp mature at 2 years to 3 years and 12 inches to 17 inches in length. Before spawning, carp move into shallow water when water temperatures reach 60 F. Generally, carp form groups consisting of one female and several males. They spawn without apparent modesty, releasing thousands of tiny eggs the size of small buckshot along shallows and vegetated backwaters. The eggs attach to vegetation until larvae hatch and are fully developed.

Carp are long-lived and fast-growing. In captivity, they may live 50 years. In Washington, carp as old as 20 years and more than 40 pounds have been reported. Carp are a nuisance where they increase the turbidity of the water and uproot aquatic vegetation that provides cover or food for native fish populations. Once established, carp are difficult to control except by non-selective poisoning methods such as rotenone.

Carp are active fish. They cruise in large schools near the water surface and often jump out of the water, causing much commotion. They are omnivores and feed throughout the water column, relying on taste and sight. Carp often can be seen in schools slurping where floating matter collects at the water's surface. Listen carefully and you may hear a soft smacking sound. A high percentage of their diet is plant material and detritus that they sort using a large pad on the roof of their mouth. Carp also eat aquatic insects, clams and snails.

A fishing license is not required to fish for carp, and there is no catch or size limit. Because carp are wary, bow fishing and spearing is also popular. Carp provide good sport by hook-and-line and can be taken by jigging and bait. "Dough-balls" are considered the best bait. Recently, Northwest fly fishermen have added carp to the list of piscine challenges. Being one who does not favor introduced species, I hope that catch-and-release of carp is not the next fad. They are considered by some to be good-eating if skinned and the dark flesh is trimmed out.

Goldfish, *Carassius auratus* (introduced). Another common name in some areas is golden carp.

Distinguishing Characteristics

Goldfish may possess a spine in both its dorsal and anal fins, but, in contrast to carp they have no barbel on the corners of the jaw. Goldfish may range from greenish to yellowish orange.

Life History and Behavior

Goldfish have established themselves in small ponds and lakes throughout the Columbia Basin. There is an occasional report of goldfish in the Columbia River, most likely the result of someone setting a pet free. They have not been as successful as carp in establishing themselves in regional waterways.

Similar to carp, goldfish spawn in shallow, marshy areas when water temperatures reach 55 F to 60 F. Breeding males have tubercles on their gill covers and anterior of their pectoral fins. Adhesive eggs are broadcast to the water column and attach to vegetation. They hatch in eight to 10 days at water temperatures of 60 F to 70 F. Goldfish are not likely to get bigger than 10 inches long in the wild.

Young goldfish eat microscopic plants and animals. Larger fish are omnivorous, feeding mostly on aquatic and terrestrial insects, scuds and plant material. Goldfish provide no benefit in natural environments, although I know that great blue heron enjoy the ones in my mother's backyard fish pond.

Tench, *Tinca tinca* (introduced)

Distinguishing Characteristics

Tench have a single pair of maxillary barbels. Their scales are small; they have more than 100 in their lateral line, so their skin appears "slick." Tench have a distinct oblique shape to their mouth.

Life History and Behavior

Tench were introduced to Pacific Northwest waters in the late 1800s. They are uncommon in the Columbia Basin except for upper Columbia River reservoirs and lakes of northeastern Washington state. Tench inhabit shallow areas of lakes and ponds, and backwaters of large rivers, generally in proximity to dense patches of aquatic vegetation.

Little is known of tench life history. They reportedly spawn in May and June. Their eggs are adhesive and attach to aquatic plants. Tench may live from 10 years to 20 years and attain weights of 10 pounds.

Tench are omnivorous. Young tench eat microscopic plants and animals. Larger tench eat aquatic plants, insect larvae and molluscs. Feeding tench leave a trail of fine bubbles behind as they swim through the water.

Tench have a unique habit of hibernating in bottom mud during the winter.

They also will estivate in the same fashion should a pond dry up in the summer. Because of their low abundance, tench have limited value as a sport fish.

Chiselmouth, *Acrocheilus alutaceus* (native). Other common names include squaremouth and hardmouth.

Distinguishing Characteristics

An unusual Northwest species of minnow is the chiselmouth, so called because of the hard, cartilaginous plate on its lower jaw having a straight, beveled edge shaped much like a carpenter's chisel. Young chiselmouth have a distinct narrow caudal peduncle and broad, flaring caudal fin. The characteristic mouth shape is well-developed by the time they are 2 inches in length. Hybridization occurs between chiselmouth and northern pikeminnow, yielding offspring with intermediate characteristics.

Life History and Behavior

Chiselmouth are found throughout the Snake and Columbia river systems, large tributaries and lakes of northeastern Washington. They often exhibit an upriver spawning run in late May and early June at Mid-Columbia River dams. Chiselmouth spawn from May to June at water temperatures of 55 F to 64 F. Spawning is mainly limited to tributaries of the Columbia and Snake rivers. Both sexes mature at 4 years to 5 years and at about 10 inches long. Maximum size is 12 inches to 14 inches.

Chiselmouth feed mainly on periphyton or attached algae. They use their stiff lower lip to scrape algae and small insect larvae from the tops and sides of river cobble. These small scrapings can be seen in nearshore areas during periods of reduced flow. Chiselmouth also have been observed feeding on green algae "blooms" in reservoirs of the Mid-Columbia.

Chiselmouth are not actively sought by sport fishermen, but they will strike a spinner or take bait and they put up a good fight. Chiselmouth are harvested for subsistence by the Nez Perce Tribe in tributaries to the Clearwater River in Idaho.

Northern pikeminnow, *Ptychocheilus oregonensis* (native). Other common names include squawfish, boxhead and yellow belly. Northern pikeminnows are a highly predacious minnow found throughout the Columbia Basin. A closely related species from the Colorado River was known to reach lengths of 5 feet.

Distinguishing Characteristics

Northern pikeminnows have large toothless mouths with the maxillary, or jawbone, extending to the front edge of the eye. The mouth has no barbels. The head is moderately long, ranging to about 23 percent of their total length. Small pikeminnows have a characteristic black spot at the base of their tail.

Life History and Behavior

Northern pikeminnows are found throughout the Columbia and Snake rivers, in larger tributaries and lakes. Juveniles occur in dense schools in low-velocity areas along the shoreline often in association with juvenile redside shiner and sucker. Adults tend to inhabit areas of slow to moderate current and are active in the upper part of the water column. Pikeminnows may migrate seasonally.

Pikeminnows spawn in June and July at water temperatures of 57 F to 65 F. Breeding males have small tubercles on the top of the head, a dark lateral band that extends from the snout to the base of the caudal fin, and yellow or yellow-orange paired fins. Pre-spawning behavior includes swarming and chasing of females by males. Eggs are gelatinous and adhesive and deposited over gravel or rocks along the shoreline. Hatching occurs in about a week at water temperatures of 59 F to 68 F.

Northern pikeminnows grow at the rate of 2 inches to 3 inches a year until they reach maturity at age 4 to 5. They may grow to weights of 5 pounds and attain 24 inches in length.

Small pikeminnows feed mainly on aquatic and terrestrial insects. Adults are opportunistic. They feed on crayfish, insects and fish. Pikeminnows readily strike lures and flies, but are passive once hooked. Their predacious behavior is well-documented, with perhaps the first description by Louis Agassiz, noted Harvard ichthyologist, in 1855: "The species of *Ptychocheilus* are among the most voracious of the whole family of Cyprinoids, exceeding probably all others in their rapacious dispositions."

In 1990, a bounty was initiated on northern pikeminnows to reduce their numbers because they prey on juvenile salmon and steelhead. This program, supported under the Northwest Power Planning Council's Fish and Wildlife Program, has effectively reduced the population size of northern pikeminnows and is thought to have increased the survival of juvenile salmonids. It seems ironic, however, that this native predator is targeted for removal while introduced predators with similar feeding habits are managed and protected for sport fisheries.

Redside shiner, *Richardsonius balteatus* (native). Other common names include Columbia River minnow, red-sided bream and silver shiner.

Distinguishing Characteristics

Redside shiners are more deep-bodied than other local minnows and have a small, slightly oblique mouth. The anal fin is comparatively long with generally more than 13 soft rays.

Life History and Behavior

Redside shiners are restricted to North America mainly west of the Rocky Mountains. They are abundant in lakes and streams throughout the Mid-Columbia. Redside shiners tend to move in large schools, ranging throughout the water column. They are often active in pelagic (offshore) areas feeding at the surface during dawn and dusk.

Redside shiners mature at 2 years to 3 years and 3 inches to 4 inches in length. Breeding males are distinctive, exhibiting red and gold stripes on their sides. Redside shiners may home to streams where they spawn from June to July at water temperatures of 58 F to 64 F. Their eggs are adhesive and usually broadcast at night over gravel bottoms or vegetated shorelines. Young-of-the-year shiners are often found schooling with northern pikeminnows and suckers in shallow, vegetated areas.

Redside shiners may attain 6 years of age and 6 inches in length. Greatest growth rates occur during the first year of life. Fry feed on zooplankton and algae. Larger shiners eat mainly terrestrial and aquatic insects along with some plant material.

Redside shiners are a forage fish of some value. They serve as food for larger, predacious fishes like northern pikeminnows, walleye and bass. They also compete with rainbow trout in some areas.

Peamouth, *Mylocheilus caurinus* (native)

Distinguishing Characteristics

Peamouth have an auxiliary process at the origin of pelvic fins and a small barbel at the corner of their mouth. The tail is deeply forked and the head relatively short, 15 percent to 17 percent of the total length. Mature fish have two dark lateral bands on their sides, often with a reddish tinge.

Life History and Behavior

Peamouth are abundant throughout the Columbia Basin in lakes, streams and reservoirs. They are generally found near the bottom and over a range of depths. Peamouth are unique among populations of native minnow by being somewhat tolerant of salt water.

Peamouth spawn over gravel or rubble bottom from late May to early June at water temperatures ranging from 52 F to 59 F. Breeding males have red lips, a bright-reddish stripe along the sides and belly, and tubercles on their heads. Eggs are adhesive and hatch in seven to eight days at 54 F.

Peamouth fry are common along shallow, vegetated areas of lakes and rivers. Young-of-the-year are usually larger than redside shiner and northern pikeminnow fry because adults spawn a few weeks earlier. Growth during the first three to four years is rapid, 2 inches to 3 inches per year, then declines at maturity or at about 10 inches in length. Maximum age of peamouth is estimated to exceed 10 years.

Small peamouth feed on zooplankton and aquatic insect larvae. Larger fish feed on larval and adult insects, snails and periphyton.

Peamouth provide limited sport value but are edible. The Washington state angling record was a 14.5-inch, 1-pound fish taken from the Columbia River.

Longnose dace, *Rhinichthys cataractae* (native)

Distinguishing Characteristics

The snout of longnose dace overhangs a subterminal mouth. They are somewhat unique in having a frenum, where the upper lip is attached to the snout providing an incomplete groove between the mouth and snout, and a thick caudal peduncle.

Life History and Behavior

Longnose dace occur throughout the Columbia and Snake river systems and are especially common in streams. They are found near the bottom in swift water, often among rocks and boulders. Dace can be seen darting about in small streams when flows are reduced in the summer. They are attracted to fine material displaced when one wades along the bottom and are not so shy as to be readily observed by a casual snorkeler.

Longnose dace spawn in June to July at water temperatures above 53 F. They broadcast eggs over gravel and rubble of shallow riffles. Eggs hatch in seven to 10 days at water temperatures of 60 F. Young dace are pelagic upon hatching, then transition to benthic or bottom habitat at about 4 months of age.

Longnose dace mature at 3 years. They are slow-growing but may get as large as 4 inches long at 5 to 6 years of age. Their food consists primarily of zooplankton, aquatic insect larvae and algae.

Longnose dace have no sport value. However, they serve as forage for predatory fish and birds and have been used as baitfish.

Speckled dace, *Rhinichthys osculus* complex (native)

Distinguishing Characteristics
Speckled dace have a terminal mouth with no frenum. The caudal peduncle is short and the rays of pelvic fins are not bound to body with "stays" of skin.

Life History and Behavior
Speckled dace are found throughout the Columbia and Snake river systems, more commonly in tributary streams. They occupy a wide range of habitats, including pools and riffles.

Spawning occurs from June through August when water temperatures approach 60 F. Breeding males have a red-orange mouth, and the base of the anal and pelvic fins are also red-orange. Adhesive eggs are broadcast in a riffle area and adhere to rocks.

Speckled dace mature at 2 years. They are short-lived and have a maximum length of 4 inches. Speckled dace feed mainly on bottom-dwelling organisms, including aquatic insect larvae, zooplankton and algae.

Speckled dace have some value as a forage fish. They are used as baitfish in areas where this practice is legal.

Two other dace, leopard dace (*R. falcatus*) and Umatilla dace (*R. umatilla*), might occasionally be found in the Mid-Columbia region. Both the leopard and Umatilla dace can be distinguished from longnose dace by virtue of not having a frenum and from speckled dace by having a more inferior mouth. The pelvic fin stays of leopard dace are most conspicuous when compared to related species. All four species have similar size and feeding habitats. All dace have subtle differences in spotting pattern, location of the mouth and pelvic fin attachments, and their scale counts overlap. Both the leopard and Umatilla dace are listed as Washington State Species of Concern because of their unknown status.

Other minnows worthy of mention but having limited distribution in the Columbia Basin include fathead minnow (*Pimephales promelas*), tui chub (*Gila bicolor*), grass carp (*Ctenopharyngodon idella*) and Oregon chub (*Oregonichthys crameri*).

- Fathead minnow are rare, occurring mostly in private ponds. They are about 2 inches long and have a robust body with a blunt nose. Their common name is derived from the thick pad that develops on the head of breeding males. Fathead minnows are a common test fish used for experimental study of toxicants and effects on fishes.
- Tui chub are thought to occur only within lower Crab Creek in Washington. They have a thick caudal fin, large scales and may grow to 10 inches in length. Populations inhabiting nearby inland lakes were eliminated following rotenone treatment. Tui chub are a common forage fish in central Oregon, but have no value as sport fish due to their small size. They are found mostly in reservoirs, ponds and slow-moving habitats.
- Oregon chub have limited distribution in the lower Willamette River system. They are protected under the Endangered Species Act due to low numbers and declining habitat. Adults are less than 4 inches long and distinguished from similar-sized minnows by virtue of large scales (less than 40 on lateral line) and a minute barbel on the maxillary.
- Grass carp were selectively released into lakes and ponds of Oregon and Washington as sterile triploids to control the growth of aquatic vegetation. However, there were recent sightings of grass carp migrating past Columbia and Snake river dams. They may reach 10 to 20 pounds. Grass carp can be distinguished from common carp by their short dorsal fin (seven to eight rays) without a spine-like ray at the front edge. They have large scales but lack maxillary barbels. It is illegal to capture and transport grass carp without a permit.

Suckers – Family Catostomidae

Suckers are an important yet widely misunderstood member of local fish communities. They are abundant throughout the Columbia Basin, have little value as consumptive or sport fishing quality, yet are an important member of the aquatic ecosystem. Although suckers adapt to many environments, their presence does not indicate poor water quality. They may compete with some game fish populations, but are more likely part of other fishes diet. Although considered resident fish, suckers may migrate several miles to spawn, including up tributary streams. There are four species of suckers in the Columbia Basin. All have inferior, or down-turned, mouths with large, fleshy lips.

Largescale sucker, *Catostomus macrocheilus* (native). Other common names include coarsescale sucker and Columbia sucker.

Distinguishing Characteristics

The number of scales along the lateral line of largescale suckers ranges from 62 to 80. Their head is relatively long, about four times in the body length. The dorsal fin is longer than it is high, with 13 to 15 rays. Their lower lip is broad and deeply incised (cleft). Largescale sucker are blackish to dark olive gray or brown on the back and side, with a yellowish to white belly. Breeding males have a thick, black band along their lateral line.

Life History and Behavior

Largescale suckers were the most abundant resident fish species collected in the Hanford Reach during comprehensive studies conducted in the 1970s. Juvenile largescale suckers are most common along shorelines in late summer and fall. Adults occur at all depths throughout the Hanford Reach, main stem reservoirs and tributary streams. Populations are transient. Greatest seasonal movement in the main stem Columbia River occurs in April at water temperatures of 46 F to 48 F.

Largescale suckers may move into tributaries of the Columbia and Snake rivers to spawn or remain in the main stem where there is sufficient current. Most spawning occurs from April through June at water temperatures ranging from 50 F to 59 F. Mature males have wart-like bumps, or nuptial tubercles, on the anal fin and lower lobe of the caudal fin during spawning.

Male largescale suckers usually mature when they reach 16 inches and 6 years to 7 years of age. Females mature at 16 inches to 18 inches and 6 years to 9 years of age. Females are larger, reaching 27 inches and 6 pounds.

The diet of largescale suckers is primarily algal periphyton and insect larvae. They are opportunistic feeders, grazing on the tops of river cobble, slurping surface debris and filtering soft bottom material.

Because of their abundance, largescale suckers are prey for other fishes such as white sturgeon, walleye, channel catfish and smallmouth bass. Suckers are also important food for predatory birds, including bald eagle, great blue heron and American white pelican. Suckers provide good spot action on light tackle. A nightcrawler with a few split shot cast in 4 feet or 5 feet of slow-moving water is usually productive. The flesh of largescale suckers is firm, white and has good flavor, although it is bony. I once smoked up several fillets of largescale suckers with a batch of mountain whitefish. When served to friends, they couldn't tell the difference.

Bridgelip sucker, *Catostomus columbianus* (native). Other common names include small-scaled sucker.

Distinguishing Characteristics

Scales along the lateral line of bridgelip suckers are small, ranging from 88 to 124. The head is about one-fifth of the body length. They have 12 to 13 dorsal rays. The lower lip is rounded and only partly cleft. Bridgelip suckers are brown to olive on the back and sides with a white belly. Breeding males exhibit a narrow, reddish-orange band along the lateral line. Hybridization between bridgelip and largescale suckers occurs and may lead to taxonomic confusion.

Life History and Behavior

Bridgelip suckers are found in similar habitat as largescale suckers in the main stem Columbia and Snake rivers. They are also abundant in tributaries, migrating into the Yakima, Walla Walla and other local rivers to spawn in the spring.

Bridgelip suckers spawn in the Columbia River from mid-April to mid-June at water temperatures ranging from 46 F to 57 F. Mature males have tubercles, or wart-like projections, in the anal fin and lower lobe of the caudal fin during spawning.

Most bridgelip suckers mature at 14 inches in length and 6 years of age. The largest reported specimen of 21 inches long was taken from the Yakima River.

Bridgelip suckers feed almost entirely on attached algae or periphyton obtained by grazing on river cobble. They may incidentally consume aquatic invertebrates, mainly insect larvae. Because of their feeding habits, bridgelip suckers are rarely taken on hook and line. However, an aggressive one may occasionally strike a spinner.

Mountain sucker, *Catostomus platyrhynchus* (native)

Distinguishing Characteristics
This species has a distinct notch at the lateral junctures of upper and lower lips. The edge of the lower jaw has a cartilaginous biting sheath and is truncated. Dorsal fin rays are usually 10; scales are small, 80 to 85 in the lateral line. They often have dark bars on their sides. Mountain suckers rarely exceed 8 inches in length.

Life History and Behavior
Mountain sucker are the smallest and least common of all local suckers. They are mostly restricted to tributaries of the Columbia River at higher elevations. Their life history and habitat use has not been well-characterized.

Males typically mature at 2 years to 3 years and 4 inches in length. Females mature at 3 years to 4 years and 6 to 7 inches. They spawn in riffles of swift mountain streams in June and July at water temperatures ranging from 52 F to 66 F.

The food of the mountain sucker is almost entirely algae and diatoms scraped from rocks. Because of their small size and feeding habits, they exist largely unbeknownst to the average angler. Mountain suckers are listed as a species of concern in the state of Washington because of unknown status.

Longnose sucker, *Catostomus catostomus* (native). Other common names include red sucker, black sucker and sturgeon sucker.

Distinguishing Characteristics
Scales are relatively small, 95 to 115 in the lateral line. The lower lip is completely cleft (incised or split in the middle) and there is no notch on the side of their mouth. They have two rows of papillae on the upper lip. Breeding males have a rosy stripe along the side. Their body color ranges from dusky brown to dark olive on the sides with a white belly.

Life History and Behavior
Longnose suckers have the northernmost and broadest natural range of all North American suckers. In the Columbia Basin, they are found in the Pend Oreille and Spokane rivers, and in Lake Roosevelt of northeastern Washington. Longnose suckers spawn in the spring in riffle areas of rivers and tributary streams of lakes at water temperatures around 41 F. Their adhesive eggs are broadcast over gravel.

After hatching, fry may remain in the gravel before moving to shallow nearshore areas to rear.

Males mature at age 4 and females at age 5 when they are 12 inches to 16 inches long. Longnose suckers have been reported as large as 30 inches and 7 pounds. They are relatively long-lived. Some females may attain 10 years of age.

Longnose suckers are bottom feeders and have a variable diet. They feed mainly on plant material, insect larvae and small crustaceans.

Longnose suckers have little value as a sport fish. Their meat is bony but said to be sweet-tasting. In some areas they are fished commercially, and their frozen fillets are marketed as "mullet."

Catfishes – Family Ictaluridae

Catfishes are readily identified by four pairs of long barbels that extend from their upper and lower jaws. These sensory appendages help them locate food and compensate for small eyes. Catfishes are smooth-bodied with no scales. They have an adipose fin and a strong, spine-like ray in front of both the dorsal and pectoral fins. Catfishes also can respire through their skin. This behavior allows them to stay alive in a wet gunny sack for an hour or more.

There are three groups of Ictaluridae in the Columbia Basin. None are native. True catfishes are large-bodied with forked tails; bullheads are smaller with square tails; and the smallest version, madtoms, have a long adipose fin that may be connected to a rounded caudal fin. In general, catfishes prefer slower water, such as reservoirs and backwaters of the Snake and Columbia rivers. They migrate into the lower reaches of large tributaries that warm up rapidly in the spring to spawn.

Channel catfish, *Ictalurus punctatus* (introduced). Other common names include spotted catfish and northern catfish.

Distinguishing Characteristics
Channel catfish are the only established member of the family having spots and a deeply forked tail. The upper jaw protrudes over the lower. The anal fin has 24 to 29 rays and a rounded outer margin. Chin barbels are pigmented. Their sides are often spotted except in very young and very old fish.

Adult male channel catfish in breeding condition are dark blue on the upper body and whitish blue on the belly, thus may be mistaken for blue catfish (*Ictalurus furcatus*). Although blue catfish were once stocked into the Snake River, there is no evidence they became established. Blue catfish are distinguished by having 30 to 36 anal fin rays and white chin barbels. The flathead catfish (*Pylodictis olivaris*) is purported to be in the lower Yakima River in limited numbers.

Life History and Behavior

Channel catfish were introduced into the western United States as early as 1874. They naturally reproduce in the Snake and Columbia rivers and lower sections of soft-bottom tributaries such as the Walla Walla, Yakima and Palouse rivers. They rarely migrate upstream of Priest Rapids Dam in the Columbia River. Snake River reservoirs have relatively higher densities of channel catfish than the Columbia River.

Channel catfish favor warm water temperatures, mud bottoms and seldom are found in dense aquatic vegetation. They have been stocked in a number of Washington lakes in the last decade in an attempt to increase predation on overabundant forage fish populations and to add diversity to mixed-species fisheries. Sprague Lake is one example of a successful application of this strategy.

Channel catfish spawn in early summer at water temperatures above 75 F. They prefer dark areas, such as undercut banks, rocks or hollow logs for spawning. They often migrate considerable distances to spawn. The male selects and clears a nest site and secretes a mucous substance to make a smooth surface. After the female has completed spawning, the male guards and fans the eggs until they hatch.

Channel catfish are long-lived and attain a large size. Both sexes mature at 3 years to 4 years of age. Males are generally younger than females for a given size.

Channel catfish feed mainly at night and twilight periods. They are omnivorous. Young catfish eat mainly insect larvae. Larger catfish eat crayfish, vegetation, aquatic insects and fish. Channel catfish are a predator of juvenile salmon and steelhead where ranges overlap.

Channel catfish are widely sought by sport fishermen. They mainly take bait – nightcrawlers, chicken liver, cut bait – fished near the bottom, but they will also occasionally strike spinners or plugs. They are caught by an illegal method of handfishing known as tickling in the southern part of the United States. Channel catfish are strong fighters and have excellent flesh quality that may be strong-flavored due to high oil content. Removing the red muscle from the midpoint of the sides moderates the taste of larger fish. The Washington state record was caught from a backwater pond in Yakima County and weighed 36 pounds, 3 ounces. The Oregon record of 36.5 pounds was from McKay Reservoir in 1980.

Brown bullhead, *Ameiurus nebulosus* (introduced)

Distinguishing Characteristics

Brown bullheads have strong barbs, or serrations, on the back edge of their pectoral spines. They lack jet black membranes between the paired fin rays and have pigmented chin barbels.

Life History and Behavior

The brown bullhead became established in the lower Columbia River during the late 19th century. It is the most common bullhead species present in ponds, lakes, sloughs and backwaters of the Columbia and Snake rivers. Brown bullheads usually reside in deeper water in the daytime and move into shallow, weedy areas to feed at night. They are tolerant of high water temperature and low dissolved oxygen.

Bullheads spawn from April to July at water temperatures of 65 F to 70 F. They make a saucer-shaped nest in shallow water, generally in mud or sand bottom, and under a log or in vegetation. At times a nest burrow is built. Before spawning the pair may "butt" one another and rub barbels. Spawning takes place in a head-to-tail position in which the caudal fin of the male is wrapped around the head of the female. Fanning the eggs is necessary because the eggs have a gelatinous coating that restricts the flow of oxygen. The male guards the nest and remains with the young until they are 1 inch to 2 inches long. Young bullheads remain in a tight school after they leave the nest and sometimes form dense "clouds" near the surface.

Brown bullheads mature at 3 years when they are 8 inches to 10 inches long. They live to 7 years, grow to 12 inches to 14 inches and reach 1 pound to 2 pounds.

Food is searched out by means of the barbels using the senses of taste and smell. This allows bullhead to feed successfully in murky or turbid water. Adult bullhead feed on just about everything found on the bottom of waterways, including clams, insects, crayfish, plant material, fish eggs and fishes.

A commercial fishery once existed for brown bullheads in the lower Columbia

River near Portland and in Idaho within lakes of the Coeur d'Alene River system. Brown bullheads readily take a variety of bait. A popular recreational fishery exists in Moses Lake and Sprague Lake. Best success is obtained by still fishing on the bottom with worms, shrimp, liver or cut bait during periods of low light. The flesh of bullheads is firm, pinkish and delicious when fried or smoked.

Yellow bullhead, *Ameiurus natalis* (introduced)

Distinguishing Characteristics
Yellow bullheads have white chin barbels and usually 25 to 26 anal fin rays. Their caudal fin is more rounded when compared to other bullheads.

Life History and Behavior
Yellow bullheads were introduced from the southeastern United States into the Columbia River in the early 20th century. They are common in Moses Lake and the Potholes Reservoir, but not abundant elsewhere. They prefer warm, clear water and rooted aquatic vegetation.

Yellow bullheads generally mature at 2 years to 3 years. Spawning occurs in May and June in a manner similar to that described for brown bullhead. They grow faster than black bullhead and may reach 18 inches in length and 2 pounds in weight.

Yellow bullheads feed opportunistically on the bottom. Primary food items include insects, crustaceans, snails, plant material and fishes. Anglers most often take them using bait. The flesh is white and reportedly delicious.

Black bullhead, *Ameiurus melas* (introduced)

Distinguishing Characteristics
Black bullheads are distinguished from yellow bullheads by having pigmented chin barbels and from brown bullheads by lacking barbs on the posterior edge of the pectoral fin spine. Black bullheads have 16 to 23 anal fin rays, and the membranes between fin rays is jet black.

Life History and Behavior
Black bullheads also were introduced into the Columbia River in the early 20th century. They prefer ponds, sloughs and backwaters of reservoirs. Black bullheads are more tolerant of high water temperature, low dissolved oxygen and poor water

quality than other catfishes.

The spawning habits of black bullheads are similar to that described for other bullheads. They typically reach 12 inches and may weigh up to 2 pounds. Bullheads mature at 2 years to 4 years and the maximum age is 6 years.

Black bullheads are omnivorous and eat insect larvae, crustaceans, snails and plant material. They bite readily on bait and are good-eating. Fish should be skinned before cooking.

Tadpole madtom, *Noturus gyrinus* (introduced)

Distinguishing Characteristics
The madtom is the smallest catfish in the Columbia Basin. It has an enlarged head and tapering body that resembles a large tadpole. It is unique in that its adipose fin is attached to and continuous with the caudal fin. Madtom range in color from dull yellow to olive gray. The tips of their lower chin barbels may be white.

Life History and Behavior
Tadpole madtoms were first introduced into Idaho from eastern and central North America. They are sometimes common in nearshore areas of the lower Snake River. They typically inhabit slow-moving, clear water, such as backwaters and sloughs, with soft mud bottoms and extensive vegetation. Empty tin cans reportedly provide attractive habitat for madtoms.

Tadpole madtoms spawn in the summer in cavities. Their eggs are light yellow, adhesive and contained in a gelatinous envelope. Maximum age is 2 years to 3 years and maximum size is 4 inches to 5 inches in length. Madtoms are sight feeders and forage mainly at night. Their diet is zooplankton and aquatic insect larvae.

Tadpole madtoms have venom-producing glands that open through pores at the base of their dorsal and pectoral spines. A puncture wound by the spines should be treated because it can lead to a secondary infection.

Killifishes – Family Cyprinodontidae

There is only one member of this family in the Columbia Basin.

Banded killifish, *Fundulus diaphanus* (introduced). Other common names include killy, topminnow and barred minnow.

Distinguishing Characteristics
Their premaxillaries are protractile. They have a rounded tail and dusky or dark vertical bars along the side.

Life History and Behavior
Killifishes are common in sloughs and other slow-moving waters of the lower Columbia River downstream of Bonneville Dam. They are tolerant of brackish conditions and can reportedly live in wet vegetation for several days. One story relates to their ability to survive after being kept among leaves in a tin can.

Killifishes are short-lived and relatively fast-growing. They may mature after 1 year and 2 inches. The maximum size rarely exceeds 5 inches. Killifishes have an extended spawning season at water temperatures around 70 F. They feed primarily on zooplankton and small insect larvae. Killifishes have some value as forage fish.

Live-bearers – Family Poeciliidae

With the exception of the guppy, a popular aquarium fish, there is only one member of this family in the Columbia Basin.

Western mosquitofish, *Gambusia affinis* (introduced)

Distinguishing Characteristics
Mosquitofishes are small, rarely exceeding 4 inches. Their mouth is superior, or turned upward; their caudal fins are rounded; and they have large, plate-like scales on the head.

Life History and Behavior
Mosquitofishes were likely transplanted to Columbia River backwaters near the confluence of the Snake and Columbia rivers in the 1970s and have since dispersed downstream and upstream into the lower Snake and Yakima rivers. Mosquitofishes inhabit backwaters, sloughs and other areas of low water velocity.

They prefer shallow densely vegetated areas and can tolerate water temperature as high as 100 F.

Both sexes of mosquitofish reproduce at 1 month to 2 months of age and for a period of four weeks to 10 weeks during which females have multiple broods. The anal fin of the male is modified into a slender intromittent organ called a gonopodium. They use this organ to fertilize females internally, an unusual method for fishes. Eggs develop inside the body of the female in a reproductive manner termed ovoviviparous.

Mosquitofishes have a short life span of about a year. Females may reach 2.5 inches in length. Males are smaller, rarely exceeding 1.5 inches in length.

Mosquitofishes are widely introduced for the biological control of mosquitoes. Their upturned mouth allows them to efficiently slurp larvae that reside at the water's surface. Other food items consumed include zooplankton and algae. Mosquitofishes have some value as forage fish in regional waterways.

Cods – Family Gadidae

Burbot are the only freshwater member of the cod family.

Burbot, *Lota lota* (native). Other common names include freshwater cod, ling, lawyer and eelpout.

Distinguishing Characteristics
These interesting fishes have a tubular shape much like an eel and a single beatnik-like chin barbel. They also have two dorsal fins. The first dorsal fin has about 13 rays; the second is quite long, having 55 or more rays.

Life History and Behavior
The burbot or freshwater ling is an unusual fish that inhabits deep, cold waters of lakes and rivers. Worldwide, they are restricted to northern latitudes of North America and Eurasia. In the Pacific Northwest, they are most common in upper Columbia River reservoirs and deep lakes at the head of tributaries. Burbot prefer to be near the bottom in areas of low light intensity. They are generally nocturnal and inactive in the daytime.

Burbot spawn in midwinter under the ice at water temperatures near 35 F. Spawning takes place at night in shallow bays of lakes or rivers over sandy or gravel bottoms. Their spawning behavior is unique. According to Canadian scientists W.B. Scott and E.J. Crossman, several males may join a female to form a "writhing ball about 2 feet in diameter."

Burbot are slow-growing and long-lived. They mature at age 3 years to 4 years at lengths of 14 inches to 17 inches. Individuals 19 years old have been recorded in Washington. Elsewhere in the world, burbot are reported to reach 46 inches and 75 pounds!

Young burbot feed on zooplankton and aquatic insects. Large burbot are a voracious predator and night feeder. They eat crayfish and other fishes that inhabit the same deep waters they reside in, such as kokanee and cisco.

Like their saltwater cod relatives, burbot livers are high in both vitamins A and D, and widely sought in Europe for canapes and other snacks. Their flesh is flaky and of good quality. Anglers fish for burbot in Lake Roosevelt by jigging or by baiting a series of hooks deployed in a long-line fashion. Populations are depressed in some locations due to overfishing and introduction of exotic, predatory fish species. The Washington state record of 17 pounds was taken from Palmer Lake in 1993.

Sticklebacks – Family Gasterosteidae

Sticklebacks are one of the most widespread fishes in the world. They live in both freshwater and marine environments and include anadromous forms. Sticklebacks are unique by having the ability to respond to changes in the magnetic field. There is only one stickleback species found in the Columbia Basin.

Three-spine stickleback, *Gasterosteus aculeatus* (native)

Distinguishing Characteristics
Three-spine sticklebacks are small fishes, rarely longer than 3 inches. They are well-armored, with three distinct spines in the front edge of the dorsal fin, large plates on the sides of their body, and a bony keel present along both sides of the caudal peduncle. Their mouth is small and equipped with tiny teeth.

Life History and Behavior
Three-spine sticklebacks are occupants of slow-moving lowland streams, lakes and ponds. They were reported by ichthyologists Charles Gilbert, professor of zoology

from Leland Stanford Junior University, and Barton Evermann of the U.S. Fish Commission, to be abundant in the "Walla Walla River of Wallula" during fisheries surveys conducted in 1893. Sticklebacks are common in Mid-Columbia River reservoirs but have not been reported in the lower Snake River. They were the most abundant species captured during extensive sampling of Wanapum Reservoir in 2000 to 2002.

Sticklebacks spawn from May through July. The male builds a nest of detritus that is stuck together using a glue-like fluid secreted from its kidneys. Nests are built in vegetation or on the bottom. Sticklebacks have an elaborate courtship behavior involving one male and multiple females. After collecting several egg clutches, the male guards the nest and aerates the eggs by fanning them with his pectoral fins. Eggs hatch in about a week at 64 F. Males may build another nest and repeat the process. Most three-spine sticklebacks die after spawning.

Three-spine sticklebacks live to a maximum of 4 years and 4 inches in length. Most live 1 year to 2 years and grow to 2 inches. They are sight feeders and their diet consists of small, aquatic insect larvae and microcrustaceans such as zooplankton and ostracods.

Three-spine sticklebacks are an important prey item of piscivorous birds such as tern and great blue heron. They also make an interesting aquarium fish to observe. Sexually mature fish can be induced to initiate mating behavior if presented with a decoy that resembles a member of the opposite sex.

Trout-perches – Family Percopsidae

There are only two species in this family. One is found in the Great Lakes region and the other in Pacific Northwest waterways.

Sand roller, *Percopsis transmontana* (native). Other common names include silver chub.

Distinguishing Characteristics
This odd, chubby little fish is the only species in the Pacific Northwest having ctenoid scales, an adipose fin and spines in both the dorsal and anal fins.

Life History and Behavior
The first record of sand rollers in the Columbia River was by the naturalist Carl Eigenmann who collected several specimens near the mouth of the Umatilla River

in 1892. Although sand rollers range throughout most of the lower Columbia and Snake rivers and major tributaries, they are uncommon. They occur over rock bottom at depths to 20 feet in the Hanford Reach. Sand rollers are secretive during the day, often seeking refuge in cover such as roots and undercut banks. At night they move to sandy, open habitats.

Sand rollers usually mature at 2 years to 3 years of age at about 3 inches in length. They may attain 6 years of age and 4 inches. Spawning occurs in May and July at water temperatures of 57 F to 61 F.

The principal food of sand rollers from the Hanford Reach is midge larvae. Caddisfly larvae and crustacean zooplankton are also part of their diet. Sand rollers have some value as a forage or prey species when they are abundant. Populations may be depressed by the introduction of non-native fishes such as walleye, channel catfish and smallmouth bass.

Bass and Sunfishes – Family Centrarchidae

This family includes several popular and colorful warmwater game fishes that inhabit lakes, ponds and rivers throughout the Columbia Basin. As a group, bass are more diverse in their habitat use than sunfishes, which generally inhabit areas having little current. Originally restricted to southern and eastern North America, various species have been widely introduced. All species are nest-builders. They make a shallow depression in the gravel to spawn and guard eggs and young through the first few weeks of life.

There are six species common to the Columbia Basin. All are characterized as having a deep, laterally compressed body. The dorsal fin is incompletely divided in two parts. The anterior dorsal fin has sharp spines and the posterior has soft rays. The anal fin also has spines.

Smallmouth bass, *Micropterus dolomieu* (introduced). Other common names may include black bass, brown bass, bronzeback or red-eye.

Distinguishing Characteristics

The upper jaw of smallmouth bass extends to mid-pupil, but not beyond the eye. They have 68 to 81 lateral line scales and 16 to 17 rays in pectoral fins. The shortest spine at the indentation of the dorsal fin is more than half the length of the spiny part of the dorsal fin giving the appearance of a continuous dorsal fin. Adults have a mottled appearance with dark, vertical bars on their sides. Young have a pronounced dark band on the end of their tail.

Life History and Behavior

Smallmouth bass were introduced to the Yakima River in 1925 where they spread to the Columbia River and various tributaries. Other stocking efforts have since increased their distribution throughout the region. Significant populations now occur in Banks and Moses lakes, the Potholes Reservoir, small lakes on the east side of the Cascades, throughout the Snake and Columbia river reservoirs and in the lower reaches of tributaries to the Columbia River, such as the John Day River in Oregon and the Yakima River in Washington.

Smallmouth bass prefer water temperatures of 70 F to 80 F. They can be found around cover such as rocky reefs, mixed rubble, gravel bars and steep drop-offs. Smallmouth bass do well in areas of moderate to slow current. They have well-defined home ranges but also may migrate several miles between over-wintering or rearing locations and spawning areas. Smallmouth bass mature at 3 years to 4 years or 8 inches to 12 inches and around 1 pound. Spawning occurs in the spring at water temperatures of 55 F to 65 F. Adult males have a strong fidelity to nest sites and return annually to the same location. Fry disperse from the nest to rocks and vegetation along the shore when they are about 1 inch long.

Juvenile smallmouth bass eat small crustaceans and insect larvae. Adult bass feed on large insects, crayfish and other fish, including sucker, minnow and juvenile salmon and steelhead.

Smallmouth bass are highly sought after by sport fishermen because of their fighting ability and eating quality. They are taken using live bait, spinners, jigs and topwater plugs. The angling record for Washington state was an 8-pound, 12-ounce fish caught in the Hanford Reach in 1966.

Largemouth bass, *Micropterus salmoides* (introduced). Other common names include green bass, bucketmouth, bigmouth and linesides.

Distinguishing Characteristics

The maxillary of largemouth bass extends well past the posterior margin of the eye. The shortest spine at the dorsal fin indentation is less than half the length of the longest dorsal spine. Thus, the spiny portion of their dorsal fin is almost separated from the soft rays. They have 58 to 69 scales in the lateral line and 13 or 14 rays in the pectoral fins. Most larger fish and young largemouth bass have a pronounced, dark band that runs along the length of the body.

Life History and Behavior

Largemouth bass were extensively transplanted in lakes, ponds, reservoirs and streams of Oregon and Washington during the 1890s. They are found in both free-flowing and impounded sections of the Columbia and Snake rivers and in hundreds of smaller lakes, ponds and slow-moving streams throughout the region. The most popular waters for largemouth bass in Washington include all major reservoirs of the Columbia Basin Irrigation Project.

Largemouth bass are tolerant of warmwater. They can often be found near weed beds and large, woody debris. Largemouth bass are sensitive to light and may seek overhead cover such as docks. They tend to move to deeper water and feed near the bottom during the day.

Largemouth bass often spawn in shallow bays at water temperatures of 60 F to 73 F. Depending on water temperature, young hatch in three to seven days. Fry remain in tight schools until they are about 1.5 inches long, after which they disperse from the nest site. Largemouth bass usually mature after 4 years to 5 years and at 10 inches to 15 inches. They are long-lived. Specimens up to 15 years of age have been reported.

The diet of largemouth bass fry is mainly small crustaceans and insect larvae. They become piscivorous at 3 inches to 4 inches in length. Juvenile minnow, sucker and salmon are all susceptible to predation by largemouth bass. Crayfish are also an important part of their diet.

Largemouth bass are an excellent sport fish, good-eating and can be taken on a variety of lures and bait. For some areas, largemouth bass in Washington are managed with a slot limit size regulation. This regulation allows for protection of fish old enough to spawn. The Washington state angling record of 11 pounds, 9 ounces was taken from Banks Lake in 1977.

Bluegill, *Lepomis macrochirus* (introduced). Other common names may include blue sunfish and blue bream.

Distinguishing Characteristics

Bluegills have a dark spot at the posterior base of the dorsal fin and a blue-black spot at the back flap of the opercle. Gill rakers on the first branchial gill arch are long and slender.

Life History and Behavior

Bluegills were introduced to eastern Washington in 1890 and 1891. They are usually found in warm, shallow lakes and ponds with rooted aquatic plants. Bluegills are oriented strongly to cover. Moses Lake, Sprague Lake and Potholes Reservoir have productive fisheries for bluegill. Bluegills also are commonly found in warmer backwater areas of the Columbia and Snake rivers where there is little or no current.

Bluegills mature at 2 years to 3 years and 3 inches to 4 inches in length. They spawn in the spring when water temperatures exceed 65 F. Bluegills practice colonial nesting where single nests may be built close to one another. Eggs from several females may be fertilized by a single male. Smaller, younger precocious males, called "cuck holders," may compete for nest sites with larger males, or "bulls." The male is pugnacious and protects the eggs during development, fanning with his fins to keep them aerated and clear of silt.

Newly hatched fry are protected by the male for several days until they disperse from the nest. Bluegill fry eat small crustaceans such as copepods. Larger bluegills are sight feeders that feed primarily during the daytime. They eat aquatic insects, including midge larvae and mayflies, snails, small fish and aquatic vegetation. Bluegills may live to 9 years to 10 years and attain 8 inches. They are typically under-fished. Stunting is a problem in managing populations, particularly in small lakes and ponds.

Bluegills are good fighters on light tackle, fine table fare and easy to catch on flies, small lures and bait. These classic "cane pole, bobber and worm" fishes will put a bend in a fly rod or light spinning rod. They are active in the winter and may be taken through the ice. A hand-sized bluegill generally is considered a decent fish by most anglers. The angling record for bluegill in Washington is 2 pounds, 5 ounces taken in Yakima County.

Pumpkinseed, *Lepomis gibbosus* (introduced). These little fishes have a slew of names including sunny, punky, yellow sunfish, sun bass and pond perch.

Distinguishing Characteristics
Pumpkinseeds are usually lighter in color and smaller than bluegills. Adult pumpkinseeds have an orangish-red spot at the posterior edge or flap of the opercle. Their gill rakers are short; length is less than twice the width of interspaces. Larger, mature specimens may have a colorful spotting pattern including turquoise and orange vermiculation on their cheeks.

Life History and Behavior
Pumpkinseeds were likely introduced to this region along with bass in the 1890s. They are found throughout the Columbia Basin in lakes, ponds, reservoirs and backwaters of large rivers. They often associate with bluegills in dense patches of aquatic plants but tend to spawn in shallower water.

Pumpkinseeds mature at 2 years to 3 years at 2 inches to 5 inches in length. They spawn at 60 F. Several females may spawn with a single male. Pumpkinseeds are territorial and defend their nest site at spawning. They grow slowly and don't usually reach an acceptable size for anglers. Pumpkinseeds may live to 6 years and 9 inches in length in some locations.

Pumpkinseeds eat aquatic insects, snails and crustacean zooplankton. They are scrappy fighters when taken on light tackle. They strike flies and bait with fierce abandon when protecting their nests in the spring. Catching enough for a meal can be problematic due to their small size.

Black crappie, *Pomoxis nigromaculatus* (introduced). Other common names may include crawpie, calico bass, strawberry bass, speckled bass, papermouth and moon fish.

Distinguishing Characteristics
The anal and dorsal fins of black crappies are almost equal in length. They are heavily speckled and usually have seven to eight dorsal spines. They have a large mouth with thin membranes.

Life History and Behavior
Black crappies were introduced into lakes near Spokane, Washington, in the 1890s. They are now found in reservoirs of the Columbia and Snake rivers, as well

as in various lakes and ponds throughout the Mid-Columbia region. Black crappies prefer dense vegetation over mud or sand bottoms. They are generally found in shallow water (less than 10 feet deep) in the spring, but may move to deeper water in the summer.

Crappies are the earliest spawners of the sunfish family. They spawn when water temperatures approach 55 F. Black crappies mature at 2 years to 3 years and at 7 inches to 8 inches in length. They spawn in May and early June at water temperatures ranging from 58 F to 64 F. Most crappies live to 5 years or 6 years old and may reach 3 pounds to 4 pounds.

Young crappies feed mainly on zooplankton and other microcrustaceans. They shift to aquatic insect larvae as they grow. Large crappies eat mainly small forage fish.

Crappies are schooling fishes, which means that when one fish is hooked, others are likely to be in the area. There are popular sport fisheries in waters of the Columbia Irrigation Project, including Banks Lake, Moses Lake and the Potholes Reservoir. Sprague Lake and Cold Springs Reservoir are also popular crappie fishing spots. Concerns for population decline have led to harvest restrictions for Moses Lake and Potholes Reservoir.

Black crappies are relatively easy to catch on bait or jigs and the flesh has an excellent flavor. They take a variety of lures including flies, bass plugs, streamers, spinners and small spoons. Moving the lure slowly is considered a key to success. State records for both Washington and Oregon waterways are from the east side of the Cascade Mountains and exceed 4 pounds in weight.

White crappie, *Pomoxis annularis* (introduced). Other common names may include white or silver bass.

Distinguishing Characteristics
The base of the dorsal fin on white crappies is shorter than the base of the anal fin. Like black crappies, their body is heavily speckled. White crappies generally have only five to six dorsal spines.

Life History and Behavior
White crappies occur in reservoirs and backwater of the Mid-Columbia and Snake rivers. They are often found in turbid or alkaline water conditions and are not

as widely distributed as black crappies.

White crappies mature at 2 years to 3 years and at 7 inches to 8 inches in length. Most do not live more than 6 years. Spawning occurs in the spring at water temperatures ranging from 64 F to 68 F. The male becomes darker at maturity. White crappies spawn near underwater structures or aquatic vegetation. As with other members of this family, males construct and guard the nest. Eggs hatch in two to three days and fry disperse quickly.

Young crappies eat mainly zooplankton. As they grow larger, they eat larger food items such as insect larvae and fish.

White crappies provide limited sport fishing opportunity on light tackle, but they have an excellent texture and flavor. The Washington state record of 2 pounds, 13 ounces was taken from the Columbia River in 1988.

Perches – Family Percidae

Perches differ from the bass and sunfishes (Centrarchidae) by having two separate dorsal fins and one to two spines in the anal fin. Like bass, yellow perch have ctenoid scales and their pelvic fins are placed forward near the pectoral fins. The yellow perch of Eurasia and that of North America are considered different species. There are two species from this family in the Columbia Basin.

Yellow perch, *Perca flavescens* (introduced). Other common names include lake perch and American perch.

Distinguishing Characteristics

Yellow perches are generally deeper-bodied and more compressed laterally (i.e., fatter and flatter) than walleyes. They lack canine teeth, have vertical dark bars on their sides, and have six to 10 soft rays in the anal fin.

Life History and Behavior

Yellow perches were introduced to the state of Washington from the Midwest more than 100 years ago; they quickly spread to lakes and backwater areas of large rivers. They typically travel in large schools of the same size and age. Yellow perches move shoreward in the spring for spawning and to more open, deeper water in the fall and winter. They are active all winter under the ice.

Yellow perches mature in their second year. Spawning occurs in April and May when water temperatures reach 45 F to 50 F. Males move to spawning grounds first. Females extrude their eggs at night in long, flat ribbon-like masses, typically near rooted vegetation or brush. The eggs are semibuoyant and hatch in 10 to 20 days. There is no parental care.

Young perch feed in shallow areas, primarily on zooplankton. As they grow, they switch to aquatic insects and small fish. Generally, perches live 6 years to 8 years. Growth is highest during the first two years. Females grow faster than males and achieve a larger size. A 10- to 12-inch perch from this region is considered large. Stunting often occurs in crowded populations such as enclosed ponds, and adults may never exceed 6 inches in length.

Yellow perch are still taken commercially in parts of North America. A record 72 million pounds of yellow perch was harvested from the Great Lakes in 1934. They are popular in local waterways because they readily take bait and lures. On a numerical basis, they contribute more to the annual catch than all other warmwater species from this region. Banks Lake, Moses Lake and the Potholes Reservoir support the most productive perch fisheries. Perch meat is white, firm and mild-flavored. Thus, they are the fish dinner of choice for many anglers. There is no size or bag limit for yellow perch except in areas where they are considered important game fish or a critical forage species. To help determine how many to keep for a meal, consider that a 7-inch perch yields two bite-size fillets.

Walleye, *Sander vitreus* (introduced). Other common names include pickerel, yellow pike and pike-perch, among other variations along the same theme. Although sometimes erroneously called "walleyed pike," they are not a close relative to pike. Part of the confusion may be related to the fact that both species have large, sharp teeth.

Distinguishing Characteristics
Walleyes have two sharp canine teeth on the tip of their lower jaw, and they attain a larger size than yellow perch. They have 12 to 13 rays in the anal fin. The lower lobe of the tail or caudal fin has a white margin. The eyes are large and have an odd, opaque look. In contrast to yellow perch, walleyes lack prominent, dark vertical bars on the sides of the body.

Life History and Behavior
In Washington, walleyes were first reported from Banks Lake and Lake Roosevelt in the early 1960s. They have since expanded their range downstream

to the Columbia River estuary and upstream to the lower Snake River. Walleyes also have been introduced widely in several lakes in eastern Washington, including Sprague Lake, Moses Lake, Soda Lake and Potholes Reservoir. Walleyes travel in loose schools, often for long distances. They generally reside near the bottom over gravel and rubble mixed with sand.

Walleyes spawn early in the spring at water temperatures of 38 F to 44 F. Males arrive on spawning grounds first. Adult walleyes spawn over sand or silt bottoms and usually at night. Each female is attended by two or more males. Eggs are adhesive initially, then become free-floating after water hardening. Fry hatch in 21 days at 50 F to 55 F. They feed on zooplankton and change to insect larvae as they grow. Walleyes are highly piscivorous, converting to a fish diet by the time they reach 6 inches in length. In the Columbia Basin, they eat minnows, sucker, sculpin and juvenile salmonids.

Walleye production is somewhat limited in lower Columbia River reservoirs due to low springtime temperatures and fluctuating water levels. Much of the recruitment occurs from upstream sites. This is because walleyes need warm backwater areas adjacent to spawning areas to ensure larval survival. Examples of suitable rearing habitat include the Spokane River arm of Lake Roosevelt and backwater side-channels of John Day pool in the lower Columbia River. Survival of larvae is poor at water temperatures less than 50 F. Walleyes have limited abundance upstream of Ice Harbor Dam in the Snake River.

Walleyes reach a catchable size of 16 inches at 4 years to 5 years old. They may reach lengths of 3 feet or more and up to 23 pounds in weight. Males mature at a younger age than females and are generally smaller. Walleyes from the lower Columbia Basin generally grow faster than other North American populations.

Popular sport fisheries for walleyes exist in Lake Roosevelt, Banks Lake, Potholes Reservoir, Moses Lake and Sprague Lake. John Day Reservoir supports an important sport fishery in the lower Columbia River. Special regulations are in effect for many waters, including a minimum size and limits on the number of larger specimens that may be kept. Walleyes are commonly taken by trolling spinner blade rigs with nightcrawlers or by jigging on the bottom. They are generally light biters. The most productive angling periods are at dawn and dusk. One reason for this behavior is that the special light-gathering layer of tissue in the back of their eyes, the "tapetum lucidum," allows walleyes to find prey at low light levels.

Walleyes are not considered strong fighters. The battle has been described as retrieving a large pair of underwear. However, walleyes taste excellent and are well worth the time spent fishing for them. The Washington state record of 19 pounds, 3 ounces was taken from the Columbia River in 2007. The Oregon record of 19 pounds, 15 ounces was also from the Columbia River.

Sculpins – Family Cottidae

Sculpins are a peculiar group of fish found throughout a wide range of freshwater and marine environments. When I fished Blue Mountain streams as a boy, my best friend called sculpins "Johnny-Behind-the-Rock." This term related to their habit of hiding in the crevices of rocks. Other anglers refer to this group of fishes as bullheads, although sculpins are not related to catfish.

Sculpins are unique in lacking an air bladder to adjust their position in the water column. Instead, they rest on the bottom of rivers and lakes using oversize pectoral fins to propel themselves upward and forward by quick strokes. Sculpins have a mottled brown and black coloration that allows them to blend in with the bottom of the river and employ a lay-and-wait strategy for capturing unsuspecting prey. Their mouth is large relative to their body length, which is an advantage for a small predator.

I provide life history information on the five most commonly encountered species of sculpins in the Columbia Basin. Many species are sufficiently rare that only a trained taxonomist can tell them apart. Please refer to Bond (1963, 1994) for more details on sculpin identification. Prickly sculpins are the only local species aggressive enough to strike a baited lure. All freshwater sculpins are edible. However, unlike their ocean-dwelling cousin the cabezon, freshwater sculpins have no value as sport fish due to their small size.

Prickly Sculpin, *Cottus asper* (native)

Distinguishing Characteristics
Prickly sculpins are the most common and largest freshwater member of the family Cottidae. The name comes from having tiny scales with ctenii, or flaps, that feel rough when you rub your finger along the side of their body. The second dorsal fin is quite long, usually with 20 or more soft rays. They have well-developed palatine teeth in the roof of their mouth and a single pore at the tip of the chin.

Life History and Behavior

Prickly sculpins are found throughout the Columbia River and backwaters, but are uncommon in the lower Snake River. They typically inhabit waters of slight current. Prickly sculpins are often associated with rubble and boulder but also are found over sandy bottom. Juveniles are found near vegetation in shallow water. Larger individuals are found at all depths.

In the spring, prickly sculpins deposit a cluster of adhesive eggs on the underside of large rocks. Eggs hatch in 11 days to 24 days at 50 F to 59 F. Larval sculpins are pelagic: They have a larval form that drifts in the water column as "ichthyoplankton" for the first month of life before they metamorphose into a more robust adult shape. Fry feed on plankton and aquatic insect larvae. Larger sculpin feed on bottom-dwelling organisms such as midge and caddisfly larvae. They also prey on small fish, including juvenile salmon. Prickly sculpins may reach lengths up to 9 inches.

Torrent sculpin, *Cottus rhotheus* (native)

Distinguishing Characteristics

The head of torrent sculpins is relatively large, greater than 30 percent of standard length. They have a narrow caudal peduncle and 14 to 17 anal fin rays. The mouth is wider than the body width at the intersection of the pectoral fins. They have two or three vertical bars that slant obliquely forward on the side of the body under the second dorsal fin. Torrent sculpins have two median chin pores.

Life History and Behavior

Torrent sculpins are found throughout the Columbia River and tributaries. They occupy areas of swift current in association with rubble and boulder cover. There are no reports of this species from the lower Snake River. They are most often found in medium to large streams.

Torrent sculpins mature at 2 years and 2 inches to 3 inches in length. They may reach 6 inches in length, although 3 inches to 4 inches is a more common size. Torrent sculpins spawn in the spring. They deposit adhesive eggs in clusters of 15 eggs to 50 eggs under rocks and logs where they are protected by the male.

In contrast to prickly sculpins, torrent sculpins lack a pelagic, or open-water, early life history stage. Eggs hatch into a form resembling the adult. Young-of-the-year sculpins eat zooplankton and insect larvae. Larger specimens eat aquatic insect larvae and fish.

Paiute sculpin, *Cottus beldingi* (native)

Distinguishing Characteristics
Paiute sculpins lack palatine teeth. The dorsal fin is usually separated to the base. They have two chin pores. Most Paiute sculpins have four pelvic fin rays.

Life History and Behavior
Paiute sculpins may be found in tributary streams of the Columbia River, such as the Yakima River, often in association with the torrent sculpins. They have been reported in the Hanford Reach but not in the lower Snake River. Typical habitat is in areas of current and near cobble or rubble bottom. They usually hide deep in the interstices between rocks.

Paiute sculpins spawn in the spring at water temperatures of 50 F. Spawning males are distinct, having a pale yellow spot on the caudal peduncle nearer the posterior margin of the second dorsal fin. They mature at 3 years, live to 5 years, and grow to 5 inches in length. Paiute sculpins eat a wide range of food items, mainly crustaceans and insect larvae.

Margined sculpin, *Cottus marginatus* (native)

Distinguishing Characteristics
Margined sculpins have 15 to 17 anal fin rays and three rays in pelvic fins.

Life History and Behavior
Margined sculpin are confined to cooler headwater tributaries of the Columbia River drainage in the Blue Mountains. They tend to inhabit pools and slower-moving water of small streams such as the Walla Walla, Umatilla, Touchet and Tucannon rivers where maximum water temperatures are less than 66 F. Margined sculpins are listed as "sensitive species" in Oregon and Washington because little is known of their status and due to degradation of habitat.

Margined sculpins spawn in May and June at water temperatures of 55 F to 61 F. Eggs are deposited under rocks and males guard the clutch. Margined sculpins feed on aquatic invertebrates such as crustacean zooplankton and insect larvae. They may reach a total length of only 3 inches.

Mottled sculpin, *Cottus bairdi* complex (native)

Distinguishing Characteristics

This sculpin may have three vertical bars under the second dorsal fin. The caudal peduncle is stout; its width greater than 18 percent of head length. The *bairdi* complex has a high morphological variability throughout their range and are often confused with other species of sculpin. Recent taxonomic evidence suggests this complex includes two separate species: *C. hubbsi* and *C. benirei*.

Life History and Behavior

Mottled sculpins are found in Columbia River tributary streams flowing from the east slope of the Cascade Mountains. They also occur in main stem reaches of the upper Columbia River, lower Snake River and Yakima River. Mottled sculpin are sedentary, having a small home range. They are often found in association with gravel and rubble. They are mainly nocturnal, feeding in open areas at night and seeking cover during the day.

Mottled sculpin mature at 2 years of age. Breeding males appear black in color and have a bright orange margin on the first dorsal fin. They spawn from May to June at water temperatures ranging from 39 F to 58 F. Mottled sculpin may live to age 7 and reach 4 inches to 5 inches in length. Their food is mainly invertebrates, including aquatic insects, and occasionally fish.

Four other, less common species of sculpins might be encountered in the Columbia River system:

- Reticulate sculpin, *Cottus perplexus* (distribution limited to the lower Columbia River and coastal streams).
- Shorthead sculpin, *Cottus confusus* (occur mainly at higher elevations of streams that originate in eastern slopes of the Cascade Mountains, such as Yakima River upstream to the Methow River. They also occur in the Kettle River in northeastern Washington and central Oregon).
- Slimy sculpin, *Cottus cognatus* (distribution limited to Lake Chelan system and upper Columbia River tributaries).
- Coastrange sculpin, *Cottus aleuticus* (distribution in the Columbia Basin is limited to the lower Columbia River downstream of Bonneville Dam).

•••

References

Chapter 1

Becker, C.D., 1990, *Aquatic Bioenvironmental Studies: The Hanford Experience 1944-84*, Studies in Environmental Science 39, Elsevier Science, Amsterdam, 308 p.

Bryant, F.G. and Z.E. Parkhurst, 1950, "Survey of the Columbia River and its Tributaries-Part IV. Area III. Washington Streams from the Klickitat and Snake Rivers to Grand Coulee Dam, with Notes on the Columbia and its Tributaries above Grand Coulee Dam," U.S. Fish and Wildlife Service Special Scientific Report – Fisheries No. 37, Washington, D.C., 108 p.

Buechner, H.K., 1953, "Some Biotic Changes in the State of Washington, particularly during the Century 1853-1953," *Research studies of the State College of Washington*, v. 21, p. 154-192.

Dauble, D.D., T.P. Hanrahan, D.R. Geist and M.J. Parsley, 2003, "Impacts of the Columbia River Hydroelectric System on Main-Stem Habitats of Fall Chinook Salmon," *North American Journal of Fisheries Management*, v. 23, p. 641-659.

Ebel, W.J., C.D. Becker, J.W. Mullan and H.L. Raymond, 1989, "The Columbia River – Towards a Holistic Understanding," p. 25-219 in D.P. Dodge, ed., Proceedings of the International Large River Symposium, *Canadian Special Publication of Fisheries and Aquatic Sciences* 106.

Geist, D.R., 1995, "The Hanford Reach: What Do We Stand to Lose?" *Ilahee*, v. 11, p. 130-141.

Hughes, R.M., R.C. Wildman and S.V. Gregory, 2005, "Changes in the Fish Assemblage Structure in the Main-stem Willamette River, Oregon," *American Fisheries Society Symposium*, v. 45, p. 61-74.

Meinig, D.W., 1995, *The Great Columbia Plain. A Historical Geography, 1805-1910*. University of Washington Press, Seattle, Washington.

Natural Research Council, 2004, "Managing the Columbia River: Instream Flows,

Water Withdrawals and Salmon Survival," National Academies Press, Washington, D.C.

Nisbet, J., 1999, *Singing Grass Burning Sage*. Nature Conservancy of Washington, Graphics Arts Center Publishing, Portland, Oregon, 119 p.

Neilson, R.S., 1950, "Survey of the Columbia River and its Tributaries Part V," U.S. Fish and Wildlife Service Special Scientific Report – Fisheries No. 38, Washington, D.C. 41 p.

U.S. Army, 1952, Columbia River and Tributaries, Northwestern United States, Volume VII, Appendix M, Coordinated Water Use Development, 81st Congress, 2d Session. House Document No. 531, U.S. Government Printing Office, Washington, D.C.

Wissmer, R.C., J.E. Smith, B.A. McIntosh, H.W. Li, G.H. Rees and J.R. Sedell, 1994, "A History of Resource Use and Disturbance in Riverine Basins of Eastern Oregon and Washington (early 1800s-1900s)," *Northwest Science*, v. 68, p.1-35.

Chapter 2

Craig, J.A. and R.L. Hacker, 1940, "The History and Development of the Fisheries of the Columbia River," *Bulletin of the Bureau of Fisheries*, v. XLIX, Bulletin No. 32, p. 133-216.

Chapman, D.W., 1986, "Salmon and Steelhead Abundance in the Columbia River in the Nineteenth Century," *Transactions of the American Fisheries Society*, v. 115, p. 662-670.

Dauble, D.D. and D.G. Watson, 1997, "Status of Fall Chinook Salmon Populations in the Mid-Columbia River, 1948-1992," *North American Journal of Fisheries Management*, v. 217, p. 283-300.

Donaldson, J.J. and F.K Cramer, 1971, *Fishwheels of the Columbia*, Binford & Mort, Portland, Oregon, 119 p.

Hunn, E.S., 1989, *Neh' I-Wana "The Big River" Mid-Columbia Indians and Their Land*. University of Washington Press, Seattle, Washington, 378 p.

Keyser, J.D., 1992, *Indian Rock Art of the Columbia Plateau*, University of Washington Press, Seattle, Washington, 139 p.

Lampman, B.H., 1946, *The Coming of the Pond Fishes*. Binford & Mort, Portland, Oregon, 177 p.

Landeen, D. and A. Pinkham, 1999, *Salmon and His People: Fish and Fishing in Nez Perce Culture*, Confluence Press, Lewiston, Idaho.

Morris, S., 1975, "The Lamprey at Kettle Falls," *Beaver*, Autumn: 18-19.

Moulton, G.E., ed., 1983, *The Journals of the Lewis & Clark Expedition*, University of Nebraska Press, Lincoln and London, v. 5, 6, 7, 9 and 11.

Oregon Department of Fish & Wildlife and Washington Department of Fisheries, 1989, Status Report. Columbia River Fish Runs & Fisheries, 1960-88, 105 p.

Schalk, R.F., 1986, "Estimating Salmon and Steelhead Usage in the Columbia Basin before 1850: The Anthropological Perspective," *NW Environmental Journal*, v. 2, p. 1-29.

Schoning, R.W., T.R. Merrill Jr. and D.R. Johnson, 1951, "The Indian Dip Net Fishery at Celilo Falls on the Columbia River," Oregon Fish Commission Contribution No. 17, Portland, Oregon, 43 p.

Smith, C.L., 1979, *Salmon Fishers of the Columbia*, Oregon State University Press, Corvallis, Oregon, 117 p.

Stewart, H., 1977, *Indian Fishing: Early Methods on the Northwest Coast*, University of Washington Press, Seattle, Washington, 182 p.

Tratzer, C.E. and R.D. Scheuerman, 1986, *Renegade Tribe*. WSU Press, Pullman, Washington, 224 p.

U.S. Department of the Interior, 1942, "Report on the Sources, Nature and Extent of the Fishing, Hunting and Miscellaneous Related Rights of Certain Indian Tribes in Washington and Oregon Together with Affidavits Showing Locations of Usual and Accustomed Fishing Grounds and Stations," Office of Indian Affairs, Los Angeles, California.

Walker, D.E. Jr., 1992, "Productivity of Tribal Fishermen of Celilo Falls: Analysis of the Joe Pinkham Fish Buying Records," *Northwest Anthropological Research Notes*, v. 26, p. 123-135.

Walker, D. E. Jr., 1993, "Lemhi Shoshone-Bannock Reliance on Anadromous and Other Fish Resources," *Northwest Anthropological Research Notes*, v. 27, p 215-250.

Walker, Deward E., Jr., volume ed., 1998, *Plateau*. Volume 12 in W.C. Sturtevant, general ed., Handbook of North American Indians, Smithsonian Institution, Washington, D.C., 791 p.

Chapter 3

Agassiz, L., 1855, "Synopsis of the Ichthyological Fauna of the Pacific Slope of North America, Chiefly from the Collection made by the U.S. Expl. Exped. Under the Command of Captain C. Wilkes, with Recent Additions and Comparisons with Eastern Types," *American Journal of Science*, v. 10, p. 71-95 and 215-231.

Burroughs, R.D., ed., 1961, *The Natural History of the Lewis and Clark Expedition*, Michigan State University Press, Lansing, Michigan.

Butler, V.L., 2004, "Where Have All the Native Fish Gone?" *Oregon Historical Quarterly*, v. 105, p. 438-463.

Dauble, D.D., 2005, "Adventures in Ichthyology," Columbia, v. 19, p. 18-23, Washington State Historical Society.

Evermann, B.W., 1896a, "A Preliminary Report upon Salmon Investigations in Idaho in 1894," *Bulletin of the U.S. Fish Commission*, v. 15, p. 253-284.

Evermann, B.W., 1896b, "Salmon Investigations in the Headwaters of the Columbia River, in the State of Idaho, in 1895," *U.S. Fish Commission Bulletin*, Article 2, p. 149-202.

Evermann, B.W. and S.E. Meek, 1897, "2. A Report upon Salmon Investigations in the Columbia River basin and Elsewhere on the Pacific Coast in 1896," *Bulletin of the United States Fish Commission*, p. 15-84.

Fulton, L.A. 1968. "Spawning areas and abundance of Chinook salmon (*Oncorhynchus tshawytscha*) in the Columbia River basin – past and present." U.S. Fish and Wildlife Service, Special Scientific Report, Fisheries 571, Portland, Oregon.

Gilbert, C.H. and B.W. Evermann, 1894, "A Report upon Investigations in the Columbia River Basin, with Descriptions of Four New Species of Fishes," *Bulletin of the United States Fish Commission*, v. 1, p. 169-207.

Girard, C., 1857, "Researches upon the Cyprinoid Fishes Inhabiting the Fresh waters of the United States of America, West of the Mississippi Valley, from Specimens in the Museum of the Smithsonian Institution," in Proceedings of the Academy of Natural Sciences of Philadelphia, v. VIII, p 165-213, 1856.

Hunn, E,S., 1980, "Sahaptin Fish Classification," *Northwest Anthropological Research Notes*, v. 14, p. 1-19,

Jordan, D.S. and Gilbert, C.H., 1882, *Synopsis of the Fishes of North America*, Government Printing Office, Washington, D.C.

Moulton, G.E., ed., 1983, *The Journals of the Lewis & Clark Expedition*, University of Nebraska Press, Lincoln and London, v. 1.

National Park Service, 1982, *Exploring the American West 1803-1879*, Handbook 116, U.S. Department of Interior, Washington, D.C.

Nisbet, J., 2005, *Mapmaker's Eye: David Thompson on the Columbia Plateau.* WSU Press, Pullman, Washington, 180 p.

Ross, A., 2000, *Adventures of the First Settlers on the Oregon or Columbia River, 1810-1813*, Oregon State University Press, Corvallis, Oregon, 319 p.

Schultz, L.P. and A.C. DeLacy, 1935, "Fishes of the American Northwest," *Journal of the Pan-Pacific Research Institution*, v. X, p. 365-380.

Schultz, L.P., 1936, "The Spawning Habits of the Chub, *Mylocheilus caurinus*, a forage fish of some value," *Transactions of the American Fisheries Society*, v. 65, p. 143-147.

Snyder, J.O., 1895, "The fishes of the coastal streams of Oregon and northern

California," *Bulletin of United States Fish Commission*, v. XIV, 1894, p.155-185. Government Printing Office, Washington, D.C.

Stevens, I.I., 1860, "Explorations and Surveys for a Railroad Route from the Mississippi River to the Pacific Ocean, 1853-55," War Department, v. XII, Book I, Thomas H. Ford Printer, Washington, D.C.

Stuart, R., 1995, *The Discovery of the Oregon Trail. Robert Stuart's Narratives of His Overland Trip Eastward from Astoria in 1812-13*, P.A. Rollins, [Ed]. Reprinted from 1935 edition, University of Nebraska Press, Lincoln and London, 391 p.

Suckley, G., 1861, "III. On the North American Species of Salmon and Trout," p. 91-160. Part II. Report of The Commission for 1872 and 1873, United States Commission of Fish and Fisheries, Washington: Government Printing Office.

Suckley, G., 1861, "Notices of Certain Species of North American Salmonids," *Annals of the Lyceum of Natural History of New York*, v. 7, p. 306-313.

Townsend, J.K., 1999, *Narrative of a Journey across the Rocky Mountains to the Columbia River, and a Visit to the Sandwich Islands, Chile, & c., with a Scientific Appendix*, Oregon State University Press, Corvallis, Oregon, 290 p.

Chapter 4

Bond, C.E., 1996, *Biology of Fishes*. Thomson Learning. Second Edition, 750 p.

Cushing, C.E. and J.D. Allan, 2001, *Streams: Their Ecology and Life*, Academic Press, San Diego, California, 366 p.

Dauble, D.D., T.L. Page, and R.W. Hanf, Jr. 1989. "Spatial Distribution of Juvenile Salmonids in the Hanford Reach, Columbia River." *Fishery Bulletin* 87(4):775-790.

Diana, J. S., 1995, *Biology and Ecology of Fishes*, Biological Sciences Press, Cooper Publishing, Carmel, Indiana, 441 p.

Wooton, R.J., 1990, *Ecology of Teleost Fishes*, Chapman and Hall, New York, 404 p.

Chapter 5

Bone, Q. and N.B. Marshall, 1990, *Biology of Fishes*, Chapman and Hall, New York, 253 p.

Moyle, P.B. and J.J. Cech, Jr., 1996, *Fishes: An Introduction to Ichthyology*, Third Edition, Prentice Hall, New Jersey, 590 p.

Schreck, C.B. and P.B. Moyle, 1990, eds., *Methods for Fish Biology*, American Fisheries Society, Bethesda, Maryland, 684 p.

Rand, G.M. and S.R. Petrocelli, eds., 1985, *Fundamentals of Aquatic Toxicology*, Hemisphere Publishing, Washington, D.C. 666 p.

Stober, Q.J. and R.E. Nakatani, 1992, "Water Quality and Biota of the Columbia River System," p. 53-83, in *Water Quality in North American River Systems*. C.D. Becker and D.A. Neitzel, eds., Battelle Press, Columbus, Ohio.

Warren, C.W., 1971, *Biology and Water Pollution Control*, W.B. Saunders, Philadelphia, 434 p.

Chapter 6

Bond, C.E., 1994, *Keys to Oregon Freshwater Fishes*, Department of Fish & Wildlife, Oregon State University, Corvallis, Oregon, 53 p.

Brown, C.J.D., 1971, *Fishes of Montana*, Big Sky Books, Montana State University, Bozeman, Montana, 207 p.

Cailliet, G.M., M.S. Love and A.W. Ebeling, 1986, *Fishes. A Field and Laboratory Manual on their Structure, Identification, and Natural History*, Wadsworth Publishing, Belmont, California, 194 p.

Carl, G.C., W.A. Clemens and C.C. Lindsey, 1973, *The Fresh-Water Fishes of British Columbia*, British Columbia Provincial Museum Handbook No. 5, Victoria, B.C., Canada, 192 p.

Schultz, L.P., 1936, Key to the Fishes of Washington, Oregon, and Closely Adjoining Regions, *University of Washington Publications in Biology*, v. 2, p. 103-228.

Simpson, J.C. and R.L. Wallace, 1982, *Fishes of Idaho*, University Press of Idaho. Moscow, Idaho, 238 p.

Wydoski, R.S. and R.R. Whitney, 2003, *Inland Fishes of Washington*, American Fisheries Society, Bethesda, Maryland and the University of Washington Press, Seattle, Washington, Second Edition, 322 p.

Chapter 7

Bond, C.E., 1994, *Keys to Oregon Freshwater Fishes*, Department of Fish & Wildlife, Oregon State University, Corvallis, Oregon, 53 p.

Carl, G.C., W.A. Clemens and C.C. Lindsey, 1973, *The Fresh-Water Fishes of British Columbia*, British Columbia Provincial Museum Handbook No. 5, Victoria, B.C., Canada, 192 p.

Nelson, J.S., E.J. Crossman, H. Espinosa-Perex, L.T. Findley, C.R. Gilbert, R.N. Lea and J.D. Williams, 2004, *Common and Scientific Names of Fishes from the United States, Canada and Mexico*, American Fisheries Society Special Publication 29, Bethesda, Maryland, Sixth Edition, 386 p.

Schultz, L.P., 1936, Key to the Fishes of Washington, Oregon and Closely Adjoining Regions, *University of Washington Publications in Biology*, v. 2, p. 103-228.

Simpson, J.C. and R.L. Wallace, 1982, *Fishes of Idaho*, University Press of Idaho. Moscow, Idaho, 238 p.

Wydoski, R.S. and R.R. Whitney, 2003, *Inland Fishes of Washington*, American Fisheries Society, Bethesda, Maryland and the University of Washington Press, Seattle, Washington, Second Edition, 322 p.

Chapter 8

Anonymous, 2005, "Warmwater Fishes of Washington," Washington Department of Fish and Wildlife Report #FM93-9.

Becker, C.D., 1973, "Food and Growth Parameters of Juvenile Chinook Salmon, *Oncorhynchus tshawytscha*, in central Columbia River," *Fishery Bulletin* v. 71, p.

387-400.

Behnke, R.J., 1992, *Native Trout of Western North America*, American Fisheries Society Monograph 6, American Fisheries Society, Bethesda, Maryland, 275 p.

Behnke, R.J., *Trout and Salmon of North America*, 2002, The Free Press, New York, 359 p.

Bond, C.E., 1963, "Distribution and Ecology of Freshwater Sculpins, genus *Cottus*, in Oregon," The University of Michigan, Ann Arbor, Michigan, 186 p.

Dauble, D.D. and D.G. Watson, 1997, "Status of Fall Chinook Salmon Populations in the Mid-Columbia River, 1948-1992," *North American Journal of Fisheries Management*, v. 17, p. 283-300.

Dauble, D.D., T.L. Page and R.W. Hanf, Jr., 1989, "Spatial Distribution of Juvenile Salmonids in the Hanford Reach of the Columbia River," *Fisheries Bulletin*, v. 87, p. 775-790.

Dauble, D.D., 1986, "Life History and Ecology of the Largescale Sucker (*Catostomus macrocheilus*) in the Columbia River," *American Midland Naturalist*, v.116, p. 356-367.

Dauble, D.D., and R. L. Buschbom, 1981, "Estimates of Hybridization Between Two Species of Catostomids in the Columbia River," *Copeia*, v. 4, p. 802-810.

Dauble, D.D., 1980, "Life History of the Bridgelip Sucker in the Central Columbia River," *Transactions of the American Fisheries Society*, v. 109, p. 92-98.

Dauble, D.D., R.H. Gray and T.L. Page, 1980, "Importance of Insects and Zooplankton in the Diet of 0-age Chinook Salmon (*Oncorhynchus tshawytscha*) in the central Columbia River," *Northwest Science*, v. 54, p. 253-258.

Gray, R.H. and D.D. Dauble, 1976, "New Distribution Records and Notes on Life-History and Behaviour of the Sand Roller, *Percopsis transmontana* (Eigenmann and Eigenmann)," *Syesis*, v. 9, p. 369-370.

Gray, R.H. and D.D. Dauble, 1977, "Checklist and Relative Abundance of Fish Species from the Hanford Reach of the Columbia River," *Northwest Science*, v. 51, p.

208-215.

Gray, R.H. and D.D. Dauble, 1979, "Biology of the Sand Roller in the Central Columbia River," *Transactions of the American Fisheries Society*, v. 108, p. 646-649.

Gray, R.H. and D.D. Dauble, 2001, "Some Life History Characteristics of Cyprinids in the Hanford Reach, Mid-Columbia River," *Northwest Science*, v. 75, p. 122-136.

Groot, C. and L. Marcolis, eds., 1991, *Pacific Salmon Life Histories*, UBC Press, Vancouver, B.C., 564 p.

Haynes, J.M. and R.H Gray, 1981, "Diel and Seasonal Movements of White Sturgeon (*Acipenser transmontanus*) in the Mid-Columbia River," *Transactions of the American Fisheries Society*, v. 107, p. 275-280.

McClane, A.J., ed., 1974, *McClane's New Standard Fishing Encyclopedia*, Holt, Rinehart and Winston, New York, 1156 p.

McPhee, J., 2002, *The Founding Fish*, Farrer, Straus and Giroux, New York, 358 p.

Mullen, J.W., M.B. Dell, S.G. Hays and J.A. McGee, 1986, "Some Factors Affecting Fish Production in the Mid-Columbia River 1934-1983," U.S. Fish and Wildlife Service Report No. FRI/FAO-86-15. 66 p.

Pacific Northwest National Laboratory, 1995, "Columbia River Salmon Mitigation Analysis System Configuration Study. Phase I. Biological Plan – Lower Snake River Drawdown," Technical Report Appendix G, Prepared for the U.S. Army Corps of Engineers, Walla Walla District, Walla Walla, Washington.

Patten, B.G. and D.T. Rodman, 1969, "Reproductive Behavior of Northern Squawfish, *Ptychocheilus oregonensis*," *Transactions of the American Fisheries Society*, v. 98, p. 108-111.

Patten, B.G., R.B. Thompson and W.D. Gronlund, 1970, "Distribution and Abundance of Fish in the Yakima River, Wash., April 1957 to May 1958," U.S. Fish and Wildlife Service Special Scientific Report Fisheries No. 603, Washington, D.C. 31 p.

Reiman, B.E., D.C. Lee and R.F. Thurow, 1997, "Distribution, Status and Likely Future Trends of Bull Trout within the Columbia River and Klamath River Basins," *North American Journal of Fisheries Management*, v. 17, p. 1111-1125.

Scott, W.B. and E.J. Crossman, 1973, *Freshwater Fishes of Canada*, Bulletin 184, Fisheries Research Board of Canada, Ottawa, 966 p.

Schultz, L.P., 1935, "The Spawning Habits of the Chub, *Mylocheilus caurinus* – a forage fish of some value," *Transactions of the American Fisheries Society*, v. 65, p. 143-147.

Simpson, J.C. and R.L. Wallace, 1982, *Fishes of Idaho*, University Press of Idaho, Moscow, Idaho, 238 p.

Vigg, S., T. Poe, L.A. Pendergast and H.C. Hansel, 1991, "Rates of Consumption of Juvenile Salmonids and Alternative Prey Fish by Northern Squawfish, Walleyes, Smallmouth Bass, and Channel Catfish in John Day reservoir, Columbia River," *Transactions of the American Fisheries Society*, v. 120, p. 421-438.

Walton, I., 1984, *The Compleat Angler*, Harrap Limited, London, 224 p.

Weisel, G.F. and H.W. Newman, 1951, "Breeding Habitats, Development and Early Life History of *Richardsonius balteatus*, a northwestern minnow," *Copeia*, v. 3, p. 187-194.

Wydoski, R.S. and R.R. Whitney, 2003, *Inland Fishes of Washington*. American Fisheries Society, Bethesda, Maryland and the University of Washington Press, Seattle, Washington, Second Edition. 322 p.

Appendix A. Glossary of Terms

adipose fin: a small, fleshy fin without rays located on the back of some fishes between the dorsal and tail fin.
ammocoete: the larval form of lamprey that lacks eyes and teeth.
anadromous: migrates from freshwater to salt water as a juvenile, then returns as an adult to spawn in freshwater.
axillary appendage: a small flap at the base of the pelvic fin of some fish.
alevin: the larval form of salmon or steelhead, from the time of hatching until the yolk sac is absorbed.
anal fin: the single fin on the ventral surface on the midline between the anus and tail.
annulus: a mark on a scale formed where circuli cross-over or compress to signify one year of growth.
barbel: a slender flexible process located near the mouth.
basibranchial (hyoid) teeth: located behind the tongue in the floor of the gill chamber.
benthic: living on or near the bottom.
branchiostegal rays: elongated bones that support the membrane below the gill cover.
canine teeth: strong, sharply pointed, conical teeth in the front part of the mouth and longer than other teeth, as in walleye and spawning salmon.
caudal fin: tail fin.
caudal peduncle: the region of the body that narrows between the anal and tail fins.
circuli: individual concentric rings on a scale.
ctenoid scale: "shovel-shaped" fish scales that have tiny indentations, or ctenii, on the exposed or posterior field; typically found on spiny-rayed fish such as bass.
cycloid scales: fish scales that are more circular in shape with a smooth exposed margin; typically found on soft-rayed fishes such as trout.
dorsal: referring to the back or upper portion of a fish.
emarginated: having a deep notch such as that found on the dorsal fin of a bass.
endangered: species in danger of extinction within all or a significant portion of its range.
eutrophic: referring to a body of water that is rich in nutrients.
fingerling: young fish; stage between a fry and adult.
frenum: fleshy bridge that connects the upper lip with the snout.
fusiform: "spindle-shaped," being broadest in the middle.

ganoid: diamond-covered scales that form an armor-type covering as in three-spine stickleback.
gill filaments: blood-filled tissue on the posterior edge of gill arches.
gill rakers: bony projections on the anterior edge of gill arches.
gonopodium: specialized, rod-shaped anal fin of male live-bearing fishes, such as mosquitofishes.
herbivorous: feeds on algae and plants.
heterocercal fin: an asymmetrical caudal fin in which the upper end of the vertebral column continues upward into the top lobe of the fin, as in sturgeons.
homocercal fin: a symmetrical caudal fin in which the vertebral column ends in a plate at its base and does not extend into the dorsal lobe, as in trout.
hybrid: a cross between two different genera or species.
hypural plate: the flattened bony region immediately anterior to the caudal fin and after the vertebrae.
isthmus: the narrow fleshy space beneath the head and between the gill openings.
kelt: a downstream migrating adult steelhead that survives spawning.
lateral line: a series of pores through scales along the midline of sides of fishes.
littoral: living along the shore of lakes and streams.
maxillary: large paired bone of the upper jaw.
melanaphores: cells in the skin that contain dark pigmentation, i.e., spotting.
metamorphosis: the change in form from one stage of development to another, as from larvae to adult.
nares: nostrils.
nuptial tubercles: sometimes called pearl organs. Small horn-like projections that form on the skin and fins of some fishes during the breeding season, as in suckers.
omnivorous: feed on both plant and animal material.
opercle: the gill plate or large, posterior flat bone that covers the gill.
oral: pertaining to the mouth.
palatine teeth: teeth on the paired palatine bones found on the roof of the mouth next to the upper jaw.
papillae: small, rounded protuberance, or nubs, on the skin or lips, as in suckers.
parr marks: vertical, dark bands found on juvenile salmon and steelhead; may persist in some adults.
pectoral fin: paired fins on the breast.
pelagic: lives in open water.
pelvic fins: paired fins on the lower side that are between the pectoral and anal fins; sometimes referred to as ventral.
pharyngeal teeth: bony projections found on and embedded in the tissues of the fifth gill arch that are used for grinding food.

phytoplankton: tiny plants.
piscivorous: fish-eating.
precocious: showing early development, such as jack salmon that mature at an early age.
premaxilla: paired bone at the front of the upper jaw that forms the edge of the jaw in most fishes.
preopercle: a sickle-shaped "cheek" bone located behind and below the eye.
pyloric caeca: finger-like blind tubes that open into the digestive tract at the junction of the stomach and intestine, as in trout.
redds: gravel nests prepared for spawning by salmon and trout.
scute: any external bony or horny plate, as in sturgeons.
semelparous: referring to salmon who complete their life cycle by dying after they spawn once.
snout: nose or part of the head anterior to the eye, but not including the lower jaw.
soft ray: a fin ray that is segmented and usually branched.
species of concern: species that are not currently listed or candidates under the Endangered Species Act but are of conservation concern within specific U.S. Department of Fish and Wildlife regions.
spine: stiff supporting structure in the front part of fins.
thoracic: of the thorax or chest.
threatened: species likely to become endangered in the foreseeable future.
truncate: having a square or broad end.
ventral: referring to the lower portion of a fish.
vermiculations: worm-like markings on the skin, as on the back of brook trout.
vomer: the bone on the roof of the mouth that is found along the midline immediately behind the premaxillaries.
zooplankton: tiny animals that live in the water column.

Appendix B. List of Fishes by Family

Taxonomic Group   **Status/Distribution**

Lampreys – Family Petromyzontidae
- Pacific lamprey, *Lampetra tridentata* .... C, W, A
- Western brook lamprey, *L. richardsoni* .... U, W, R
- River lamprey, *L. ayresi* .... U, L, A

Sturgeons – Family Acipenseridae
- White sturgeon, *Acipenser transmontanus* .... C, W, R
- Green sturgeon, *A. medirostris* .... U, L, E

Herrings – Family Clupeidae
- American shad, *Alosa sapidissima* .... C, W, A

Salmon, trout, char and whitefishes – Family Salmonidae
- Mountain whitefish, *Prosopium williamsoni* .... C, W, R
- Lake whitefish, *Coregonus clupeaformis* .... C, L, R
- Brook trout, *Salvelinus fontinalis* .... C, L, R
- Bull trout, *S. confluentus* .... C, L, R
- Lake trout, *S. namaycush* .... U, L, R
- Brown trout, *Salmo trutta* .... C, L, R
- Cutthroat trout, *Oncorhynchus clarki* .... C, W, R, E
- Rainbow trout/steelhead, *O. mykiss* .... C, L, A/R
- Chinook or king salmon, *O. tshawytscha* .... C, W, A
- Sockeye/kokanee, *O. nerka* .... C, W, A/R
- Coho or silver salmon, *O. kisutch* .... C, W, A
- Pink salmon or humpy, *O. gorbuscha* .... U, L, A
- Chum or dog salmon, *O. keta* .... U, L, A

Smelts – Family Osmeridae
- Eulachon, *Thaleichthys pacificus* .... C, L, E

Pikes – Family Esocidae
- Northern pike, *Esox lucius* .... U, L, R
- Grass pickerel, *E. americanus* .... U, L, R

Minnows – Family Cyprinidae
- Common carp, *Cyprinus carpio* .... C, W, R
- Grass carp, *Ctenopharyngodon idella* .... U, W, A
- Goldfish, *Carassius auratus* .... U, W, R
- Tench, *Tinca tinca* .... C, W, R
- Chiselmouth, *Acrocheilus alutaceus* .... C, W, R

Northern pikeminnow, *Ptychocheilus oregonensis* .... C, W, R
Redside shiner, *Richardsonius balteatus* .... C, W, R
Peamouth, *Mylocheilus caurinus* .... C, W, R
Fathead minnow, *Pimephales promelas* .... U, L, R
Tui chub, *Gila bicolor* .... U, L, R
Longnose dace, *Rhinichthys cataractae* .... C, W, R
Leopard dace, *R. falcatus* .... U, W, R
Speckled dace, *R. osculus* .... U, W, R
Umatilla dace, *R. umatilla* .... U, L, R
Oregon chub, *Oregonichthys crameri* .... U, L, R

Suckers – Family Catostomidae
Largescale sucker, *Catostomus macrocheilus* .... C, W, R
Bridgelip sucker, *C. columbianus* .... C, W, R
Mountain sucker, *C. platyrhynchus* .... U, L, R
Longnose sucker, *C. catostomus* .... C, L, R

Catfishes – Family Ictaluridae
Channel catfish, *Ictalurus punctatus* .... C, W, R
Brown bullhead, *Ameiurus nebulosus* .... C, W, R
Black bullhead, *A. melas* .... C, W, R
Yellow bullhead, *A. natalis* .... C, W, R
Tadpole madtom, *Noturus gyrinus* .... U, L, R

Killifishes – Family Cyprinodontidae
Banded killifish, *Fundulus diaphanus* .... U, L, E

Live-bearers – Family Poeciliidae
Western mosquitofish, *Gambusia affinis* .... U, W, R
Guppy, *Poecilia reticulata* .... U, L, R

Cods – Family Gadidae
Burbot, *Lota lota* .... U, L, R

Sticklebacks – Family Gasterosteidae
Three-spine stickleback, *Gasterosteus aculeatus* .... C, W, R

Trout-perches – Family Percopsidae
Sand roller, *Percopsis transmontana* .... U, W, R

Bass and Sunfishes – Family Centrarchidae
Smallmouth bass, *Micropterus dolomieu* .... C, W, R
Largemouth bass, *M. salmoides* .... C, W, R
Bluegill, *Lepomis macrochirus* .... C, W, R
Pumpkinseed, *L. gibbosus* .... C, W, R
Black crappie, *Pomoxis nigromaculatus* .... C, W, R
White crappie, *P. annularis* .... C, L, R

Perches – Family Percidae
    Yellow perch, *Perca flavescens* .... C, W, R
    Walleye, *Sander vitreus* .... C, W, R

Sculpins – Family Cottidae
    Prickly sculpin, *Cottus asper* .... C, W, R
    Torrent sculpin, *C. rhotheus* .... C, W, R
    Paiute sculpin, *C. beldingi* .... U, W, R
    Margined sculpin, *C. marginatus* .... U, L, R
    Mottled sculpin, *C. bairdi* .... U, L, R
    Reticulate sculpin, *C. perplexus* .... C, L, R
    Slimy sculpin, *C. cognatus* .... U, L, R
    Shorthead sculpin, *C. confusus* .... U, L, R
    Coastrange sculpin, *C. aleuticus* .... U, L, E

Key to Symbols: C = common; U = uncommon; W = widespread; L = limited distribution; A = anadromous; R = freshwater resident, E = estuarine

Appendix C. Tributaries and Main Stem Dams of the Columbia and Snake Rivers Within the Range of Described Fishes

Source: *River Mile Index Main Stem Columbia River* (1962) and *River Cruising Atlas: Columbia, Snake, Willamette.* (1997) Evergreen Pacific Publishing Ltd. Shoreline, Washington.

Columbia River Tributaries and Dams	River Mile
Willamette River, Oregon	101.5
Sandy River, Oregon	120.5
Bonneville Dam	146.1
Wind River, Washington	154.5
Drano Lake-Little White Salmon River, Washington	162.0
White Salmon River, Washington	168.3
Hood River, Oregon	169.4
Klickitat River, Oregon	180.4
The Dalles Dam	191.5
Deschutes River, Oregon	204.1
John Day Dam	215.6
John Day River, Oregon	218.0
Umatilla River, Oregon	288.8
McNary Dam	292.0
Walla Walla River, Washington	313.5
Snake River, Washington	324.3
Yakima River, Washington	335.2
Priest Rapids Dam	397.0
Wanapum Dam	415.0
Rock Island Dam	453.4
Wenatchee River, Washington	468.4
Rocky Reach Dam	474.5
Entiat River, Washington	483.7
Chelan River, Washington	503.3
Wells Dam	516.6
Methow River, Washington	523.9
Okanogan River, Washington	533.5
Chief Joseph Dam	545.1
Nespelem River, Washington	582.1

Grand Coulee Dam	596.3
Spokane River, Washington	643.0

Snake River   **River Mile**

Ice Harbor Dam	9.7
Lower Monumental Dam	41.6
Palouse River, Washington	59.2
Tucannon River, Washington	62.4
Little Goose Dam	70.5
Lower Granite Dam	107.4
Clearwater River, Idaho	139.4

Appendix D. Regional Web Sites Related to Fish and Fishing

Bonneville Power Administration Fish & Wildlife Group – Contains information on fish and wildlife proposals, ongoing programmatic activities and research reports. http://www.efw.bpa.gov/

Columbia Basin Research – Home page of the University of Washington for salmon migration studies on the Columbia River. Includes DART (Data Access in Real Time) where information can be obtained on adult salmon passage, smolt indices and river environment data. http://www.cbr.washington.edu

Fish Passage Center – Provides up-to-date information on juvenile salmon and steelhead passage, hatchery release schedules, temperature, flow, and dissolved gas conditions in the Columbia and Snake rivers. http://www.fpc.org/

Northwest Fisheries Science Center – Information on anadromous fish management including recent reports by the research arm of the National Marine Fisheries Service (NMFS). http://www.nwfsc.noaa.gov/

Idaho Department of Fish and Game (IDFG) – Offers a Fisheries Publications Library, planning documents, hatchery activities and fishing reports. http://www.fishandgame.idaho.gov/

Oregon Department of Fish and Wildlife (ODFW) – Data on fish and habitat data by specific river basin or geographic area and sport fishing updates. http://www.dfw.state.or.us/

U.S. Army Corps of Engineers, Northwestern Division – Current data on flows and reservoir status, fish passage data at all federal hydroelectric projects on the Columbia. https://www.nwd.usace.army.mil/home.asp

U.S. Geological Survey – Source of information for streamflow data throughout the Pacific Northwest, including daily discharge, gauge elevation and temperature. http://waterdata.usgs.gov/nwis

U.S. Fish and Wildlife Service, Region 1 – General information on endangered species. http://www.fws.gov/pacific/

Washington Department of Fish and Wildlife (WDFW) – Current news releases including sport fishing statistics. http://wdfw.wa.gov/

Washington State Department of Health – Fish Consumption Advisories. http://www.doh.wa.gov/fish/

INDEX

Italicized page numbers indicate illustrations. Color plates, located after page 118, are indicated by *cp* following the plate number.

A

age of fish, determining, 77
algae, 62, 64, 65
American perch, 164
American shad. *see also* herrings
    biology/spawning, 115–116
    branchiostegal membranes, 83
    color plate, 2*cp*
    contaminants and, 73
    introduction of, 28
    key to species, 103
    salinity and, 67
anadromous fishes, 6, 7, 27, 52, 66, 119, 123. *see also specific anadromous fishes*
anatomy, 73–80
Arctic grayling, 117
aufwuchs, 46
aurora trout, 120

B

bait, 40, 51, 130. *see also* food
banded killifish, 11*cp*, 102, 154
Barnhart, Billy, *37*
barred minnow, 154
bass. *see also* introduced species
    anatomy, 73, 75, 77, 79
    bait/food, 47, 50, 51, 55, 111
    biology/spawning, 158–160
    color plate, 12–13*cp*
    habitat, 5
    keys to family/species, 92, 102–103
bigmouth bass, 159
big redfish, 131
black bass, 158
black bullhead, 95, 152–153
black crappie, 14*cp*, 28, 102, 162–163

black sucker, 148
blueback salmon, 14, 130
blue bream, 161
blue catfish, 150
bluegill, 13*cp*, 28, 77, 103, 161
blue sunfish, 161
body parts, 73-80
bottom-feeders, 48, 50
bounties, 55
boxhead, 140
branchiostegal membranes, 83
bridgelip sucker, 10*cp*, *104*, 105, 147
bronzeback, 158
brookie, 120
brook trout, 3*cp*, 27, 96, 120-121, 122, 126
brown bass, 158
brown bullheads, 11*cp*, 95, 151-152
brown trout, 4*cp*, 98, 116, 120, 126
bucketmouth, 159
bullhead catfish, 49, 52, 151-153
bull trout, 3*cp*, 27, 40, 96, 119-120
burbot, 12*cp*, 89, 100, 155-156

C

calico bass, 162
calico salmon, 133
candlefish. *see* eulachon
care of fishes, 72
carnivores, 153
carp
    biology/spawning, 48, 137-138
    color plate, 8*cp*
    consumption safety, 69
    explorers and, 35
    fins, 81
    food, 48, 50
    history of, 25
    keys to family/species, 93, 105
    oxygen and, 62
    taste, sense of, 52

catch and release, 72, 114
catfishes. *see also* bullhead catfish; channel catfish
    anatomy, 75, 78, 81
    biology/spawning, 149–153
    contaminants, 73
    fishing strategies, 51
    history of, 28
    keys to family/species, 88, 95
Celilo Falls, *19,* 115
channel catfish, 10*cp*, 49, 55, 95, 149–151. *see also* introduced species
chars, 89, 96–100, 116. *see also* bull trout; lake trout
Chinook (king) salmon
    biology/harvest rates/spawning, 13, 19, 22–23, 25, 33, 124, 126–129
    color plate, 5*cp*
    ESA status, *27*
    explorers and, 36
    food, 61
    Indians and, 14
    key to species, 100
    migrations, 25–26, 52, 60, 63–64
    populations of, 6, 13, 22
    redds, *49*
    sport fishing, 25–26
    studies of, 43
chiselmouth, 8*cp*, 18, 39, 40, 50, 56, 105, 140
chiselmouth jack, 117
chubs, 9*cp*, *27*, 34, 39, *41*, 107, 142–143, 145, 157
chum (dog) salmon, 7*cp*, *27*, 43, 99, 133–134
circuli, 77, *78*
clams, 48
Clark, William, 32–35
climate change, 68–69
coarsescale suckers, 146
coastrange sculpins, 170
cods, 89, 100, 155–156
coho (silver) salmon
    biology/harvest rates/spawning, 22, 26, 124, 129–130
    Clark and, 33
    color plate, 5*cp*

    key to species, 99
    studies of, 43
collection of fishes, 72
coloration, body, 55, 72, 73
Columbia Basin, *1*
Columbia River, *60*
Columbia River minnow, 142
Columbia River smelt, 134
Columbia suckers, 146
commercial fishing, 18, 20–25, 26, 53, 111, 112, 114, 119, 128, 130, 149, 151
competition, 56, 64
consumption safety, 69
contamination, 67, 69. *see also* pollution
counter-current exchange, 79
counter-shading, 55–56
counting, 80, 81–82
cover, 47, 59
crawpie, 162
crayfish, 47
Crown Point State Park, Oregon, 57
currents, 54, 63
cutthroat trout, 4*cp*, 15, 27, 96, 116, 122–123, 126

D

daces, 9*cp*, 31, 40, 50, 143–145
The Dalles, 18–19, 21
dams, 4, 6–7, 9, 43, 63, 129, 188–189. *see also* fish ladders
depth measurements, 81
diatoms, 46
digestive system, 79, 82
dip nets, 14, 16, 18–19, 20, 24, 134
discharge (water flow), 59, 62–65. *see* instead pollution
diversity, 20, 65, 79, 150, 176
doctor fish, Indian, 17
dog (chum) salmon, 7*cp*, *27,* 43, 99, 133–134
Dolly Varden, 119
dragnets, 21
droughts, 64

E

eelpout, 155
"eels," 27, 110
electroreceptors, 53
elevation drop, 63, 64
Endangered Species Act (EPA), 27, 110, 120, 131, 133, 145
eulachon (candlefish). *see also* anadromous fishes
    biology/harvest rates/spawning, 24, 134
    Clark and, 33
    color plate, 7 *cp*
    Indians and, 16-17, 34
    keys to family/species, 96
    salinity and, 67
expeditions, scientific, 39-42
explorers, 32-38
extinctions, 130, 131

F

families, key to, 86-107
fathead minnow, 107, 145
fathom fish, 134
feeding behaviors, 45. *see also* mouths
filter-feeders, 50-51
fin clips, 26
fins, 74-76, 81-82
fishing. *see also* commercial fishing
    archaeological evidence, 31
    game, 28
    Indian, 14-20
    methods, 20, 51, 129, 132, 133, 150
    seasons, 18
    sport, 25-27, 34-35, 38, 40, 55, 130
    weather and, 53-54
fishing camps, 13-14
fish ladders, *44*
fish wheels, 21, *22*, 111
flathead catfish, 150
flies/lures, 34, 35, 36, 51
flooding, 64

food, 50–52, 56, 61, 64, 128, 147. *see also* bait; biology *under specific fishes*
food webs, *45*, 46–48
fork length, 81
freezing, 59–60
freshwater cod, 155
freshwater fishes, 66. *see also specific fishes*
freshwater ling, 100

G
game fish, 5
gigs, 15–16
gill arch/rakers, 82
gill nets, 20
gills, 79
golden trout, 123
goldfishes, 81, 105, 138–139
gorge, fish, *15*, 34
gradient of a stream, 63
grass carp, 145
grass pickerel, 7*cp*, 100, 136
grayling, 116, 117
green bass, 159
green sturgeon, 67, 95, 114–115
guppy, 102
guts, 78–80

H
habitat, 59
Hanford Reach, 6–7, 43, 47, 49, *54*, 56, 110
hardmouth, 140
harvest rates, 18, 22–25. *see also* biology *under specific fishes*
hatcheries, 22, 26, 40, 122
head (body part), 80
hearing, 54, 78
herbivores, 79
herrings, 36, 93, 103, 115–116, 117. *see also* American shad; mountain whitefish
hibernation, 60
homing, 52, 53
hooligan, 134

human impacts, 7-11, 8, 10, 62, 64, 67-69, 110, 129, 141. *see also* hydroelectric dams
humpback salmon, 132
humpy salmon, 6*cp*, 132
hydroelectric dams, 2, 4, 7, 8-10, 42-43, 112-113, 129, 131
hydrographs, 62-63
hydrostatic pressure, 54

I

ice, 59-60
ichthyology, 42-43
identifying fishes, 71-72, 81. *see also* keys to families/species; *specific fishes*
Indian doctor fish, 17
Indians
    conservation by, 16
    explorers and, 34, 36, 37-38
    fisheries, 25
    harvest rates, 18
    lampreys and, 111
    lifestyle, 13-20
    salmon and, *12*
insects, 47, 56, 61, 64
introduced species, 5, 9, 11, 28-29, 43, 55-57, 141. *see also specific species*
invertebrates, 47-48, 65

J

jack Chinook salmon, 36
jaws, 77
John Day Rapids, *2*
"Johnny-Behind-the-Rock," 167

K

kelt stage, 125
keys to family/species, 85-107
killifishes, 11*cp*, 91, 102, 154
killy, 154
king salmon (Chinook), 5*cp*
kip, 77
koi, 137
kokanee salmon, 5, 6*cp*, 56, 61, 82, 130, 131, 132. *see also* salmon; sockeye salmon

kype, 77

L
lake perch, 164
lakes, 5, 27, 61
lake trout, 3*cp*, 96, 120, 121–122
lake whitefish, 3*cp*, 96, *97*, 118–119
lampreys
    archaeological evidence, 31
    biology/spawning, 109–112
    categorization of, 71
    color plate, 2*cp*
    commercial fishing, 23
    Indians and, 16, 17, 20, 31, 37
    keys to family/species, 87, 94
    salinity and, 67
    studies of, 40
largemouth bass, 5, 13*cp*, 28, 80, 103, 159–160
largescale suckers, 9*cp*, 104, 146–147
lateral line, 78
lawyer, 155
lengths, 81
leopard dace, 106, 144–145
Lewis and Clark expedition, 32–35
life histories, 45. *see also* biology *under specific fish*
light, 53, 66
linesides, 159
ling, 155
little redfish, 130, 131
live-bearers, 101–102, 154
"Lonesome Larry," 131
longnose dace, 9*cp*, 106, 143–144
longnose sucker, 10*cp*, 148–149
longnose suckers, 105
lures/flies, 34, 35, 36, 51

M
macrophytes, 47

margined sculpin, 101, 169
measurements, 80–83
mechanical stimuli, 53, 54, 78
meristics, 80, 82
migration, 13, 25, 33, 52–54, 60, 64, 66–67, 129
minnows
    anatomy, 77, 79
    archaeological evidence, 31
    biology/spawning, 136–145
    identifying, 83
    keys to family/species, 93, 105–107
    migration and, 52
    predators and, 51
    studies of, 31, 39, 40, 43
mirror carp, 137
mitigation, 42–43
moon fish, 162
morphometry, 80, 81–82
mosquitofish, 11*cp*, 50
mottled sculpin, 101, 170
mountain herring, 118
mountain sucker, 10*cp*, 104, 148
mountain trout, 120, 122
mountain whitefishes
    anatomy, 75, *97*
    biology/harvest rates/spawning, 49, 116–119
    color plate, 2*cp*
    contaminants, 69
    explorers and, 36
    identifying, 82
    Indians and, 17
    keys to family/species, 89, 96
    studies of, 40
mouths, 50, 76–77
mud trout, 120
mullets, 15, 34, 35, 149

N

native fishes, 29, 43. *see also specific fishes*
non-native fishes, 28–29, 149. *see also* introduced species

northern catfish, 149
northern pikeminnow
    anatomy, *76*, 82
    biology/spawning, 48, 140-141
    color plate, 8*cp*
    food, 47, 50, 51, 55, 56
    keys to families/species, 107
    studies of, 39
northern pike, 28, 100, 135-136
nutrient loading, 67

O

observation of fishes, 72
oil, fish, 17, 18, 24-25, 37
omnivores, 50, 138, 139
opossum shrimps, 56
Oregon chub, *27*, 145
organs, internal, 51
oxygen, 59, 61-62, 67

P

Pacific lamprey, 94. *see also* lampreys
Pacific salmon, 116
Paiute sculpin, 101, 169
papermouth, 162
peamouth chub, 9*cp*, 34, 39, *41*, 42, 107, 142-143
perches, 14*cp*, 88, 91, 102, 164-167
periphyton, 56
petroglyphs, *17*
photic zones, 47
phytoplankton, 46
pickerels, 7*cp*, 165
pike-perch, 165
pikes, 89, 100, 134-135
pink salmon, 6*cp*, 99, 132-133
"Pinocchio," 117
piscivores, 50, 56, 79, 166
plants, aquatic, 47
poison, 15
pollution, 51, 67-69, 79

pond perch, 162
predators, 50, 51, 53, 55, 56, 64, 150. *see also specific predators*
premaxillaries, *106*
preservation methods, 41–42, 72
prey, 55, 60
prickly sculpin, 15*cp*, 100, 167–168
pumpkinseed, 13*cp*, 103, 162
punky, 162
pyloric caeca, 82

Q
quinnat salmon, 126

R
rainbow trout
    anatomy, *73, 82*
    availability, 5, 26–27
    biology/spawning, 123–126
    brook trout and, 120
    color plate, 4*cp*
    cutthroat and, 122
    food, 50, 56
    genetics, 116
    key to species, 98
rays, 78
redds, 49
red-eye, 158
redfish (sockeye), *41*
red salmon, 6*cp*, 130. *see also* sockeye salmon
red-sided bream, 142
redside shiner, 5, 9*cp*, 40, 48, 106, 142
red sucker, 148
regulations, 21, 25, 27, 112, 114, 138
reproductive organs, 79–80
reservations, Indian, 18
reservoirs
    discharge and, 62
    overviews, 4, 5, 9, 10
    steelhead and, 124

    studies, 43
    temperatures, 62
    white sturgeon and, 113
restoration, 42-43
reticulate sculpin, 170
rheotaxis, 54
river lamprey, 109
rivers, 3-7, *27*, 33, 37, 47, 60, 61, 188-189

S

salinity, 65, 66-67
salmon. *see also* anadromous fishes; commercial fishing; Indians; Lewis and Clark expedition; *specific types of salmon*
    anatomy, 75, 77, 82
    biology/harvest rates/spawning, 18, 21, *48*-49, 116, 124-134
    contaminants, 69
    homing, 53
    human impacts, 8, 9, 63
    Indians and, *12*, 15, 16, 18, 38
    introduced species and, 55
    keys to family/species, 89, 96-100
    migrating, 10, 11, 52, 53, 63
    oxygen and, 62
    pre-settlement, 31
    salinity and, 67
    smell, sense of, 51
    studies of, 39, 40, 42
    taxonomies , 41
    temperature and, 60
salmon leather, 133
saltwater fishes, 66
salvation fish, 134
sand roller, 12*cp*, 31, 40, 75, 95, 157-158
Snake River, 3-4, *8*
scales, 77-78, 82
science, 42-43
scientific expeditions, 39-42
scientific studies, 39, 40, 42, 43, 49, 62, 69, 111
sculpins (Indian doctor fish), 15*cp*, 17, 31, 40, 79, 89-90, 100-101, 167-170

seines, 15, 20–*21*
sensitive species, 169
set nets, 20, 21
shad. *see* American shad
sharks, 78
shorthead sculpin, 170
silver bass, 162
"silver bryte" salmon, 134
silver chub, 157
silver salmon, 33. *see also* coho salmon
silver shiner, 142
silverside, 130
silver trout, 130
slimy sculpin, 170
smallmouth bass, 12*cp*, 28, 50, 60, 69, 103, 158–159
small-scaled sucker, 147
smell, sense of, 51, 53, 128
smelts, 24–25, 88, 96, 134. *see also* anadromous fishes; eulachon (candlefish)
"smolts," 125
Snake River, 43
snowmelt, 68–69
sockeye salmon. *see also* kokanee salmon; salmon
    biology/harvest rates/spawning, 22, 130–132
    illustrations, 6*cp*, *41*
    Indians and, 14
    key to species, 99
    migrating, *27*, 52
    studies of, 43
soft rays, 75–*76*, 81
sound, 54, 78
spawning, 36, 48–50, 51, 52, 53, 65, 73. *see also specific fishes*
spears, 15–16
species/families, keys to, 85–107
Species of Concern, Washington State, 145
speckled bass, 162
speckled dace, 106, 144–145
speckled trout, 120, 122
spiny rays, 28, 75–*76*, 81
"splake," 120, 121
sport fishing, 25–27, 34–35, 38, 40, 55, 130

spotted catfish, 149
spotting patterns, 73
spring salmon, 126
squaremouth, 140
"square-mouth," 40
square-tail, 120
squawfish, 39, 140
standard length, 80–81
steelhead. *see also* anadromous fishes
    archaeological evidence, 31
    biology/harvest rates/spawning, 22, *48*–49, 123–126
    color plate, 4*cp*
    ESA status, *27*
    explorers and, 36
    fishing strategies, 64
    human impacts, 8, 9, 63, 69
    Indians and, 14
    key to species, 98
    migrating, 10, 11, 53, 63
    regulations, 26
    salinity and, 67
    studies of, 39, 42, 43
    temperature and, 60
sticklebacks
    biology/spawning, 156–157
    color plate, 12*cp*
    history, 31
    keys to family/species, 92, 103
    migration and, 53
    nests, 49
    scales, 78
stocking, 27, 125, 150
strawberry bass, 162
sturgeons. *see also* anadromous fishes
    archaeological evidence, 31
    archaeological remains, 31
    biology/harvest rates/spawning, 6, 112–114
    explorers and, 34
    fishing strategies, 51
    Indians and, 17

    keys to family/species, 87, 94–95
    photo, *24*
    scales, 78
sturgeon sucker, 148
substrate, 65
suckers
    anatomy, 73, *76*, 77, 79
    availability, 5
    biology/spawning, 145–149
    color plates, 9–10*cp*
    contaminants, 69
    food, 50, 51, 56
    history, 31, 36, 40
    identifying, 83
    Indians and, 18, 31
    keys to family/species, 93, 103–105
    migration and, 52
    salinity and, 67
    studies of, 43
    taste, sense of, 52
sun bass, 162
sunfishes
    anatomy, 73, 75, *75*, 79
    availability, 28
    biology/spawning, 49–50, 161–164
    keys to family/species, 92, 102–103
sunny, 162
Swan Falls Dam, 9
swim bladder, 79
symbiosis, 56

T

tadpole madtom, 11*cp*, 95, 153
tails, *76*, 80
taste, sense of, 52
taxonomies, *32*, 41–42, 71, 185–187. *see also* measurements
teeth, 76–77
temperatures, water
    Columbia *vs.* Snake Rivers, 37
    discharge and, 64

    feeding and, 50
    human impacts, 8, 10–11
    migration and, 53
    oxygen and, 61–62
    populations and, 59–61
    salinity and, 66
    stress, as, 67
tench, 8*cp*, 105, 139–140
"thalwag," 125
thermocline, 61
threatened species, 120, 133
three-spined sticklebacks. *see* sticklebacks
"three-toothed" (Pacific) lamprey, 40. *see also* lampreys
"tiger trout," 120, 126
topminnow, 154
torrent sculpin, 15*cp*, 101, 168
total length, 80–81
traps, 15–16, 21
treaties, 18, 20
trout
    anatomy, 73, 75, 77, 79, 82
    archaeological evidence, 31
    biology/spawning, 119–126
    fishing strategies, 53–54, 64
    food, 50
    keys to family/species, 89, 96–100
    oxygen and, 62
    studies of, 40
trout-perches, 88, 95, 157–158
trunk, 80
tui chub, 107, 145
"tule," 127
tyee salmon, 126

U
Umatilla dace, 144–145

V
vegetation, 3
velocities of water, 63, 64, 111, 113

visual cues, 51, 54

W

"walleyed pike," 165
walleyes. *see also* introduced species
    anatomy, 50, 77
    availability, 5
    biology/spawning, 165–166
    color plate, 14*cp*
    consumption safety, 69
    history, 28
    key to species, 102
    light and, 53
Wallula Gap, 14, *30*
warm-water tolerant fishes, 4, 28, 43, 69
water flow (discharge), 10, 59, 62–65
water quality, 59, 64, 67–69
weather, 53
Web sites, 190–191
weirs, *15*, 34
"wendigo," 121
western brook lamprey, 94, 111–112
western mosquito fish, 11*cp*, 154–155
westslope cutthroat trout, 122, 123
white bass, 162
White Bluffs, *6*
white crappie, 5, 102, 163–164
whitefish, 2, 3*cp*, 31
white salmon trout, 33
white sturgeon
    bait/food, 48, 111
    biology/harvest rates/spawning, 6, 23, 112–114
    categorization of, 71
    color plate, 2*cp*
    contaminants, 69
    fins, 75
    Indians and, 20
    key to species, 95
    salinity and, 67

studies of, 40

Y

Yakima River, *4*, 67
yellow belly, 140
yellow bullhead, 95, 152
yellow perch, 5, 14*cp*, 28, 48, 102, 164–165
yellow pike, 165
yellow sunfish, 162

Z

Zone 6 fishery, 25
zooplankton, 46, 56

About the Author

Dennis Dauble grew up chasing minnows and crawdads in small creeks near his home in northeastern Oregon. He parlayed those habits into a 35-year career at Pacific Northwest National Laboratory to study the life history and ecology of resident and anadromous fishes from the Hanford Reach, habitat requirements of fall Chinook salmon, and fish passage issues at Columbia and Snake River dams. He has also had the opportunity to sample fishes in faraway places such as the irrigation canals of Italy and rios of Mexico.

Dauble serves as an adjunct professor at Washington State University–Tri Cities. He earned a Bachelor of Science and doctorate in fisheries from Oregon State University and a Master of Science in biology from Washington State University. Current diversions include penning popular articles for regional fishing magazines and a regular column on the natural history of Columbia Basin fishes for the *Tri-City Herald*.

When not fishing for trout, steelhead, salmon and other fishes, he enjoys time spent restoring his vintage cabin in the Umatilla River valley and hanging out with his wife, Nancy, their two grown children (and respective spouses), and four grandchildren. Each grandchild caught his or her first trout on a fly rod during a summer stay at the cabin.